CW00971664

The Answer
You're Looking for
Is Inside of You

The Answer You're Looking for Is Inside of You

A Commonsense Guide to Spiritual Growth

Mark L. Prophet

COMPILED AND EDITED BY

Elizabeth Clare Prophet

SUMMIT UNIVERSITY PRESS®

THE ANSWER YOU'RE LOOKING FOR IS INSIDE OF YOU:
A Commonsense Guide to Spiritual Growth by Mark L. Prophet.
Copyright © 1997 by Summit University Press. All rights reserved.

No part of this book may be used, reproduced or transmitted in any
manner whatsoever without written permission, except by a reviewer
who may quote brief passages in a review. For information, write or call
Summit University Press, Box 5000, Corwin Springs, MT 59030-5000.
Telephone: 406-848-9891. Web site: http://www.tsl.org

Library of Congress Catalog Card Number: 96-069717
ISBN: 0-922729-26-3

SUMMIT UNIVERSITY 🦢 PRESS®
Summit University Press and 🦢 are registered trademarks.

This book is set in Sabon.
Printed in the United States of America
First Printing 1997

The paper used in this publication meets the requirements of the American
National Standards Institute Z39.48-1992 (Permanence of Paper).

Contents

Preface

It's not often that we find someone who can marry profound spiritual truths to the practicalities of everyday life in a thoroughly understandable and enjoyable way. Mark Prophet had that gift.

His number one rule: the spiritual quest, though challenging, should be fun. And number two: we can often find the answers we're looking for in the most unlikely places.

Mark knew that deep down inside, people are trying to find God—whether they call him the Christ or the Buddha, the Tao or Brahman. His lifelong goal was to help everyone he met realize more of that spiritual essence.

He also believed that there is a spark of the divine within each of us and that we can contact that God within. Even before it was fashionable, Mark was teaching spiritual seekers how to become mystics. The mystic believes that he can gain direct knowledge of God through subjective experience and intimate communion with the All in all.

Mark himself was a mystic. He was also a pioneer in religious thought. Raised in the Christian tradition, he later experimented with the teachings of the Eastern adepts and came to a deep appreciation of the unity of all the world's religions.

The Hindu yogi, the Taoist sage, the Buddhist monk, the

Christian mystic—he believed we could learn from them all, and he did. He was as happy meandering through the sublime passages of the Bhagavad Gītā as he was reading about the lives of the Christian saints. And he was as comfortable meeting with the Dalai Lama as he was conversing with Mother Teresa of Calcutta.

Mark knew that the adepts of the Himalayas had a profound message for him, so he made a pilgrimage to India with sixty devotees to probe the mysteries of each one's unique transcendental union with God. Though Mark had spiritual powers from childhood, he sat at the feet of gurus and holy men who practiced the secret traditions of Hinduism and Buddhism.

For more than twenty years Mark dedicated himself to teaching and publishing the wisdom of the Eastern and Western adepts. He walked with them through the pages of their writings until he became one with them. And in all of their teachings he detected the single golden thread that creates unity out of diversity: the realization that each of us can experience our own intimate relationship with God.

In the pages that follow, developed from three of Mark's lectures, you will see that his approach to spirituality is a practical one. He bases his lessons on universal spiritual laws but translates the nuances of the spirit into language we can all understand and immediately apply to our life's journey.

Teresa of Avila, a supremely practical mystic, once counseled the sisters of her order, "The Lord walks among the pots and pans." There, she said, "is where love will be seen: not hidden in corners." Mark, too, has an uncanny way of portraying, as if in bas-relief, the opportunities for spirituality that we can chisel out of the seemingly ordinary circumstances of everyday life. For he believed that that's where spirituality matters most and reveals its best face—in our daily life.

The Answer You're Looking for Is Inside of You is a commonsense guide to spiritual growth. Its insights, spiced with anecdotes and techniques for self-mastery, help us see ourselves and the world around us through new eyes.

Perhaps most importantly, it shows us how refreshing it is to laugh at our own humanness—and how ennobling it can be to weave into our daily rhythms the wisdom of our highest self. As Mark would say, it's okay to be human as long as you remember you're divine.

❧

I dedicate this book to Mark L. Prophet, my teacher, my friend, my companion, the father of our four children and the lover of my soul.

I knew Mark for twelve blessed years. He gave me so much love, so much wisdom and a sense of the universal self that impels us to the heights of our ultimate reality.

Mark's lectures are inimitable. They teach you how to break the bread of life, how to trust your deepest instincts and how to know the God within. And he transmits to you his strong spiritual tie to the adepts and Ascended Masters of the Far East, whom he knew so well.

Through Mark I came to know who I am in the present and who I could become in the eternal now. He gave me a true sense of my wholeness and he was the only man I ever met who told me he loved my soul. Until then I didn't even know that my soul had worth.

As you read Mark's many lectures or listen to him on audiocassette, you will—here subtly, and there with a big

WOW!—come to an awareness of being, your being, that no other prophet or pastor has ever been able to unlock for you.

What is Mark's secret? It is his love for all people. Because, on contact, he was acquainted with their innermost being. Mark had a magnanimous heart. He reached out to touch and heal all whom he met through the transfer of light from his heart to theirs. He read their hearts. He knew their pain. He gave comfort to the meek and wisdom to those who could hear it. Mark was and is "a man for all seasons."

Let this mystic of mystics quietly enter your heart, take you by the hand and lead you to the secret chamber of your heart. He will open the door and reveal to you the eternal flame your Maker sealed in that chamber. And he will tell you that that flame is your flame of immortality that you must tend daily with your own special prayers.

Mark Prophet is a servant of God and of the God who lives within you. At the conclusion of his final sojourn on earth, he attained union with God and became one with the immortals. If you walk with him a mile or two, he will teach you and love you until the hour of your soul's fulfillment.

Try him. Test him. You will find him to be one of your best friends on earth and in heaven.

Elizabeth Clare Prophet

A NOTE ON LANGUAGE

Because gender-neutral language can be cumbersome and at times confusing, we have often retained Mark Prophet's use of the pronouns *he* and *him* to refer to God or to the individual and his use of *man* or *mankind* to refer to people in general. We have used these terms for readability and consistency, and they are not intended to exclude females or the feminine aspect of the Godhead. For instance, the word *Man* in the title of chapter one, "Christ in the Heart of Man," includes all people.

Spiritual or esoteric terms that may be unfamiliar to some readers have been defined in a brief glossary at the end of the book.

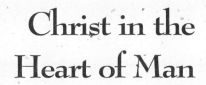

Christ in the Heart of Man

❦ *"If you cannot find the truth right where you are, where else do you expect to find it?"* —Dōgen

❦ *"Put not out the Light which hath shone forth in you. As ye see yourselves in water or mirror, so see me in yourselves."* —Jesus

CHAPTER ONE

Christ in the Heart of Man

*T*oday our hearts turn towards the Eternal Presence, and we go backward in time into the eternal consciousness and ponder the birth of the creation and the vastness of the creation.

In Sanskrit we find the word *kala,* which means "time," and the word *desha,* which means "space." Let us think, then, in terms of time and space as though time and space were a gentle bubble hovering beneath the consciousness of God.

In this bubble, in this heart of space where all things exist, there is an extraordinary beauty—a beauty that oftentimes our words or even our thoughts cannot adequately describe. For a moment we may try to grasp all of this, but it is incomprehensible to us because it extends too far and is too great.

However, we do comprehend our relationships. Within our own circle of friends and with those we feel are nearer and dearer to us, our relationships are well established. Yet the Master said, "Other sheep I have, which are not of this fold: them also I must bring."[1] So we should understand that in the consciousness of the Christ there is a spirit of gathering together rather than a tearing apart.

THE LOVE OF GOD

Let us recognize, then, the tremendous depth of God's love. It is a love that not only is now but always has been and always will be.

If we can escape from the densities of this world, God's love will enable us to find a freedom that we have never known before—freedom in consciousness, freedom in our being, dominion over our physical bodies, over our consciousness, over our mind, over our heart and over all things that surround us.

All these things belong to the heart of God, and they *are* God's. But they are also ours, because his Son has said, "I go to prepare a place for you, . . . that where I am, there ye may be also."[2] And so we begin to develop a sense not only of the love of God but also of the extension of God or the permeation of God throughout the universe.

We have failed to think in terms of what the Ascended Masters have called "hallowing space." Space was intended to be hallowed, not desecrated. Space is hallowed when it absorbs the energies of God. As a sponge absorbs water so our consciousness can absorb God's consciousness, and God's consciousness can penetrate our consciousness. And in this penetration comes a new awareness of where we are.

We see the world in both the microscopic and the telescopic. And thereby we recognize that there is a greater largess of God's heart in the universe than we had thought.

Mirrored in the faces of people around us we have seen limitation. Perhaps they are limited by a sense of sin, a sense of smallness or largeness of size, a sense of economic status. We have allowed these things to penetrate our consciousness. And we are concerned with having worldly fun—if you can call it fun.

Well, let's take a look at a new idea: Is it fun to do the will of God? That's the question. Is it fun to do the will of God?

Is it possible that the chairman of the board of the universe can have better ideas than the chairman of the board of Ford Motor Company?

Can we ingest the glow of the cosmic sense?

Can we realize what it means?

Can God come down to us and show us our own inherent worth?

God's love is ours. We belong to that love. And that love is dynamic! That love is not cheap, it is not vulgar. It is magnetic. It draws us unto itself. It reaches out through the whole universe. It is what all of us possess as the germinal spark within us.

Today, unfortunately, we live in a world of sham, a world where people dare to pull other people's strings. We have seen the world compartmented and splintered and its wholeness shattered. All of this creates degeneration.

Now, we contain the factors of generation and degeneration, whereby people are born and die. And we contain the factor of regeneration, wherein people unite with the power of immortal life.

We find that unregenerate man—ordinary man—is a bit of a disobedient child. He may not know that he is being disobedient. Yet his ignorance of the law is not a valid excuse when he stands before the heavenly magistrate.

We of ourselves can do nothing, but through Christ we can do all things. We are dealing with the Universal Christ; we are not dealing with a figment of our imagination. The life that beats our heart is no transient tramp that passes through and then is no more. True, ships may pass in the night, but we are concerned with that which we will call contact with God—*contact with God.*

"God is a Spirit," I read in John 4:24, "and they that worship him must worship him in spirit and in truth." This is regeneration. And this regeneration is a tremendous factor in the transformation of our lives.

LIFE CAN BE A BOOMERANG OR A CORNUCOPIA

God has been painted as an angry God who is eager to impale us upon a stick and then roast us as a marshmallow. I don't believe this. I believe that God is a God of love.[3]

I also believe that God is a God of exactness. As I give my energy out into the universe, so that energy will return to me. As I treat my fellowmen, as I treat my God, as I treat all of life and its wondrous opportunities, so I will be treated according to my just deserts.

Life is either a boomerang or a cornucopia. It's a boomerang if we send out bad energy; it's a cornucopia if we send out the abundant life. If we want the good life that is God's life, we must send out into the world the vibration of hope and light and beauty and strength.

The outer garments we wear are meaningless. They could be rags or riches; it wouldn't make any difference. Our outer garments are a sham unless we have something within our heart—something of the divine spark that is regenerative.

What does the Bible say on this? Jesus said some will say, "Christ is here" and "Christ is there." "Go not after them, nor follow them," he said. "For, behold, the kingdom of God is within *you.*" [4]

I have known any number of preachers, men of the cloth, who talk about how great they are—how great *they* are—but who fail to recognize the greatness in their congregations and in the masses of the people.

It is a greatness that is spread amongst us. Do you realize that? Try to realize it. Try to grasp it.

I remember as a child singing the song "Brighten the Corner Where You Are." These days life sometimes gets pretty dull. It would really help if we would remember to brighten the corner where we are. But everybody thinks the brightening will be done through television or a Broadway extravaganza or by one of the great preachers like Oral Roberts or Billy Graham. The people think the preachers are just going to get out and do it all.

Well, God is not a failure. He doesn't make mistakes. And he's been around a long time. Yet people are continuing to make mistakes. Why? Because God gave them free will and they misuse it. That's the answer, and it's the only answer.

"Well," someone says, "why doesn't God appear and forbid this or forbid that? Why doesn't he appear and say—?" He does. He does it through his laws.

Take the law of karma, for instance. In one lifetime people may do a series of wrong things and a series of right things or a combination thereof. Then God gives them another life, and circumstances become either bad or good, depending on how they treated others in their past life. And they say, "Why? Why did God do this?"

But it isn't God that has done it—we ourselves did it! We either misused our free will or we didn't, and now we find ourselves dealing with the consequences of our past actions.

Just because we made some mistakes in this life or past lives doesn't mean we can't pick up where we left off and earnestly engage in balancing our karma from both our yesterdays and our todays. We still can use our free will properly or improperly. The option is ours. We are the ones that have to decide.

CAN YOU SIN, BE FORGIVEN AND NOT HAVE TO MAKE RESTITUTION?

Now I am going to explain to you the law of karma as you have probably never heard it explained before. From the time of Christ and even before Christ, people have had a sense of guilt. People still do. And in this sense of guilt, they seek forgiveness for their sins.

Where do they seek it? They seek it from God. And they seek it from someone lesser than God, because Jesus Christ gave the power to forgive sins to his apostles and they in turn transferred that authority to the priests down through history.

Now, people have funny ideas about karma and forgiveness. They think that you can kick a man and go up to him afterwards and say, "Will you forgive me?" And the man, Christian as he is, says, "Of course I will. I realize that you did wrong, but I'll forgive you."

Then you turn to God and you say to God, "I kicked a man, will you forgive me?" And God says, "Yes, I'll forgive you." So, man has forgiven you, God has forgiven you and you feel very forgiven. And you believe that your slate is now wiped clean. But, you see, the record of your injustice is still there.

The whopping mistake that popes, priests, ministers and people have made for thousands of years is this: they don't understand that although God and man have pardoned you, the Great Law requires that you make restitution for your misdeeds. In other words, you can be forgiven immediately, but God's justice must be meted out. Your misdeeds are not wiped out simply because someone, even God, forgives your sins. For as you do unto others, so will it be done unto you.[5] That is the irrevocable law of the Great White Brotherhood.

Do you know why down through the centuries many people became Christians? They became Christians because they were told that Jesus Christ would forgive their sins— and this is true. However, they don't understand that they still have to make restitution for their sins.

In his book *Autobiography of a Yogi,* Yogananda relates

this story about the Indian master Babaji: One night, Babaji's disciples were sitting around a bonfire that had been prepared for a sacred ceremony. Suddenly Babaji grabbed a burning brand from the hot fire and lightly struck the bare shoulder of a disciple who was near the fire.

One of the master's disciples said to the master, "How cruel!" What was the master's answer? He said, "Would you rather have seen him burned to ashes before your eyes, according to the decree of his past karma?"

Then Babaji put his hand on the disciple's injured shoulder and healed him. And Babaji said, "I have freed you tonight from painful death. The karmic law has been satisfied through your slight suffering by fire."[6]

The burning the master inflicted upon the man was less suffering than otherwise would have come to him as a result of his karma. He may have burned someone to death in a past life but had since become a good man, was no doubt practicing attunement with God and was performing religious service. He was trying to find God, trying to make contact. Since he was a friend of God, his sins were not imputed unto him with the same degree of intensity as they would have been if he had not been a friend of God.[7]

People have the idea that they can do whatever they want to do with impunity. They say, "My life is my own. I'll do what I please because I believe in the doctrine of the vicarious atonement—that Jesus died for my sins."

Well, I believe that Jesus can forgive sins. I believe, for example, that Jesus Christ forgave one of the two thieves who were hanging on crosses to the right and the left of him. One of the thieves said to Jesus, "Are you not the Christ? Save yourself and us."

But the other thief said, "Do you not fear God, since you are under the same sentence of condemnation? And we indeed have been condemned justly, for we are receiving the due reward of our deeds, but this man has done nothing wrong." And he said to Jesus, "Lord, remember me when you come into your kingdom." Jesus replied, "Verily I say unto you, today you will be with me in paradise."[8]

I believe these words to be true, but I also believe that from behind the veil of paradise the thief was required to reach out in consciousness to right every wrong that he had done, just as every one of us must do.

People place great hope in their salvation through Christ's forgiveness of their sins. They say, "Oh, the Lord forgave me for every sin I ever committed," and the next day they go out and do the same thing or worse. Isn't that something! They ask for forgiveness and then they turn around and do or say the same things that they were just forgiven for.

I do not say that God cannot forgive sins, but people must remember that even if God forgives them, they still need to make amends for their sins. As the saying goes, there are no atheists in the foxholes. When men face death, they begin to recognize that there is a power greater than themselves.

It makes no difference to me whether or not you are able to accept the law I have revealed to you, because your own conscience will tell you that you must make restitution for your sins. If you can accept this law and believe that it works impartially for you and for everyone, you will be able to take more responsibility for your life.

Some people never learn to take responsibility for their lives. I was in a restaurant the other day and I overheard a woman say, "You know, everything I do is illegal or fattening or immoral." That's the way she saw herself and that's what she did. And that's the way people think. They think they can do anything and get away with it.

We must begin to realize that *all* of our acts, *all* of our thoughts, everything we do is recorded in the computer that God himself put inside of us. That computer registers our every thought and feeling both in our mind and in the mind of God.

MAKING FUN OF OUR OWN ANTICS

People can solve many of their problems, but they can't seem to solve the problem of impatience. One time I was driving down the street and the man ahead of me stopped suddenly. I blew my horn at him—until I saw a little old lady walking haltingly across the street.

Sometimes people get so mad that they're ready to kill each other because one or the other won't drive fast enough, for instance. But in our impatience, many of us are literally losing our souls.

As an adjunct to finding more of God in our lives, we need to develop the habit of patience—especially patience with ourselves. Just because you don't become a master overnight is no reason why you should give up! For goodness' sake, it took some of the Ascended Masters a thousand years to earn their ascension!

Saint Germain once told us, "I made over two million right decisions before I made my ascension." The Master did not say how many *wrong* decisions he might have made during the centuries in which he made those two million right decisions.

All of us have made mistakes. I don't know anyone who hasn't made mistakes. If people tell you that they haven't made any mistakes, you can be certain they haven't done anything of worth.

Well, I've known a few virtuous people all right. But some people have never heard of God or Christ except as swear words. Some have seen Buddha only in the form of an incense burner. As Christ took Mary Magdalene and made a saint out of her, so those who have not known God or Christ can also become saints.

Yet many times the ninety and nine believe so much in their own self-righteousness that they have no room in their being for the righteousness of God. Jesus Christ, Abraham, Saint Germain, Mother Mary, all the Ascended Masters at some time on their spiritual path made room in their being for the righteousness of God.

Now, some people say that Saint Germain is a devil. I'm not here to challenge these people, but I would like to have the opportunity to tell them that they have a misconception about Saint Germain. Saint Germain is one of the greatest and kindest and most loving friends of Jesus you'll ever find. And Saint Germain is the foremost exponent of freedom—

personal freedom, freedom for America and freedom for the world.

But how do you get freedom? Well, first you have to get free of the ego. How do you get free of the ego? You get free of the ego by being nonattached to the ego.

Silly, vain people admire themselves and their egos so much that they almost break the mirrors they look into! And if the mirrors crack, why, they say, "I am going to have seven years' bad luck." How superstitious they are! Aren't some of the things we do silly—I mean, really silly?

The seventeenth-century comic playwright Molière was a master at poking fun at people's antics. He artfully exposed the sham and hypocrisy of the Parisians of his day through his ludicrous characters.

There's the tradesman of *Le Bourgeois gentilhomme (The Bourgeois Gentleman),* who thought superficial manners, affected speech and ridiculous costumes would turn him into a gentleman. And the fake physician of *Le Médicin malgré lui (The Doctor in Spite of Himself),* who duped his client by spouting made-up Latin-sounding words and prescribing eccentric remedies. And the haughty girls of *Les Précieuses ridicules (The Romantic Ladies),* who spurned two honest and wealthy suitors because they were not dandies.

Molière made the people laugh at their pretensions, and as a result some of them even changed their ways. We should also develop the habit of making fun of our own antics, realizing that such antics are not divine at all.

Now, one of the problems of the self-styled gurus is that they're so busy courting the public and trying to build a personal following that they will not admit that all God wants is for people to discover *him.*

"Well," you say, "how am I going to discover God? Do I excavate or do I aerate? What am I supposed to do to find God?" Well, this is very silly.

A student of anatomy told me that he had dissected the human body and couldn't find God in it or even a sign of life. Naturally! The essence of God, and any sign of life, left the body when he started the dissecting process. In the same way, when a pathologist dissects the body during an autopsy and the organs are removed for examination, all that is left is the shell of the body.

So when you get through taking the body apart, there isn't anything of God left—there's just a bunch of dead tissue. Because it is the Spirit that breathes the breath of life into the body at birth, and it is the Spirit that withdraws the breath of life at the hour appointed by God. "The LORD gave, and the LORD hath taken away; blessed be the name of the LORD."[9]

MIRACLES REALLY HAPPEN

If we stopped to think about all the sins we have committed throughout our life, from the cradle to now, we might get depressed. We might say, "What chance do I have?" Well, dear hearts, remember one thing: the little lump of gold and the great mountain of dirt.

We may have a little lump of gold in our consciousness that may be covered over by a big mountain of dirt. But we are concerned with the something of worth—the lump of gold, not the mountain of dirt. One day that mountain of dirt will be changed into gold in the twinkling of an eye, when the last trump sounds.[10]

People have a mistaken idea about the last trump. They say the last trump is not going to sound during their lifetime but sometime in the future. When it happens, all at once God's going to speak and everyone who has died since the world began is going to be resurrected and Christ is going to come in the clouds with great power and glory.[11]

I guess they believe he's going to send them in two different ways, because the Bible says he will separate the sheep from the goats.[12] I believe the separation of the sheep and the goats happens every day. We all stand before the judgment seat of our Holy Christ Self every day and the great white cloud appears every day. That great white cloud is the throne of witness in nature itself.

Can you look at a cloud?

Can you hear a meadowlark sing?

Can you gaze into the face of a child?

Can you look at people and see the beautiful way in which God constructed them and the unlimited potential he placed within them, including the possibility of unlimited greatness?

Can you look at all of that and not be moved?

Can you say that there is no God, there is no balance, there is no justice in the universe? Of course you can't!

Well, the possibilities that fly within you can be yours today or tomorrow or in the future. You can have them all!

You may say, "I don't believe that." Don't fool yourself. I've had hundred dollar bills multiply right in my wallet just because I needed them. I don't know where they came from; all I know is that they appeared. That's only a little miracle. We've had greater miracles than that in our lives, and these miracles have happened to members of our organization and our friends.

"I certainly would like to have a friend that could do all these things for me," you say. Well, your God Presence and your Holy Christ Self are your friends and *they* can perform miracles. Life's not all about miracles, but the miracle of life itself is very great. Don't you think so?

SATURATE YOURSELF WITH GOD

Isn't it a wonderful thing that we can be saturated with God? Now, you take a dried-out sponge and attempt to wash the wall. What happens? Maybe it wipes off a little dust. So you mix the best solvent in the world in some water and you dip your sponge into the mixture. The sponge absorbs the water and the solvent, and then you can wash the wall with it.

Just so, you have to absorb God. It is not sufficient that God exists in the universe, that he exists in space, that he hallows space. You have to absorb God if you want to clean up your world. And we all need to be cleaned up.

"But wait a minute," you say. "I thought we were made in the image and likeness of God." And so we were. I can show you the God within yourself, but you have to make an effort to get to know him before you can learn how to externalize him. Sadly, in many of us the image of God has become a latent image. The image of God is there; you just don't see it. Sometimes you don't even feel it.

I remember going to Pennsylvania many years ago to attend a large meeting. I met all kinds of strange people there. One of the ladies said to me, "Ever since I began to know about the Masters, I just started to tingle. I tingle all over."

"Well, that's wonderful," I said. "And what does it do for you?"

Well, she didn't know what it did for her, but she knew she was tingling.

"Do you want to tingle?" I asked.

"No," she replied.

So I looked at her and said, "Well, you will tingle no more."

At four o'clock that afternoon I met her, and I asked, "Are you tingling anymore?"

"No, it's all gone," she said.

"Well," I said, "I told you this would happen and it has, because it is not necessary to tingle in order to find God."

If an Ascended Master comes into the room where you are, he can make you tingle from head to toe. You may, if you're sensitive, if you're attuned, if your spiritual sight is opened, see and feel the Master's presence.

One time I was standing on the platform in a hotel in Washington, D.C., taking a dictation. Suddenly I felt surrounded with light. I perceived the light and the light was very thick. It grew thicker until I could scarcely see the faces of the people. The room was just a sea of living light.

Then I looked down at my feet and saw that I was standing about two inches off the floor. No one else noticed it. And pretty soon, I comfortably came back to the floor and

I walked to the receiving line and greeted the guests and shook hands with them.

As they passed by, one woman said, "I don't like you."

How much effort God puts into courting people! And no matter how much he courts them, they still don't like the presence of God. They don't like the Spirit. They don't like the power of change. They'd rather sit down in their rotting corpses and rot away.

That is true. The potential for death is in us, even as the potential for life is in us. The angels of life and the angels of death are present in our consciousness. What happens depends on whether we choose to walk in God's light or to walk in darkness.

Now, I've always thought it a bit sad that the ones who know can't make the decisions for those who don't know. I talked to the Master Jesus about that, and he said to me:

"Each one must pass through the door for himself. The love of God and the grace of God are sufficient for every man and woman, but they have to discover this for themselves. What seems to you to be inefficient and a waste of cosmic energy doesn't mean very much, since we are talking about the Infinite One and his abundant life. If people want to fritter away their energy without seeking and finding God, there's nothing you can do about it, because there's nothing God can do about it." And I began to realize that.

"But," the Master said, "you can be a city set on a hill. You can be a light that cannot be hid.[13] *You* can raise up the Christ in you. And when you raise up and elevate the Christ consciousness in yourself, then I, Jesus, will draw all men unto me[14]—not unto you, but unto me." And that's the way it should be.

THE ANSWER YOU'RE LOOKING FOR IS INSIDE OF YOU

That's why we don't worship anyone's personality in this place. Oh, you can look at me as a reed shaking in the wind and you can say to yourself, "How good is he? What kind of a man is he?" You are not going to find your Creator by looking for the answer in me. It's in yourself. That's where the search begins.

You can't come into this place of worship and sit and gaze at me and thereby become a Christian or a member of the Great White Brotherhood or an adept or an Ascended Master or anything else you might want to be. But what you can do is you can learn of the appearance of Christ within your individual world. You can try to find him inside of you.

If you can't find Christ in yourself, then just keep looking, because he's there. I can assure you he's there. Keep looking within and stop looking elsewhere!

We represent the Great White Brotherhood. We can speak for them because they have given us their mantle. They conferred that authority upon both Elizabeth and me. It was not for the sake of our egos. We're not interested in praising ourselves; we're interested in praising the God who dwells within all of us and in raising people up to that God-awareness. We are interested in restoring harmony and health and wholeness in the consciousness of man.

Today let us decide for ourselves that we can discover a gold mine of consciousness within. It is the consciousness of the indwelling Christ. And when we find that consciousness, we will have a new appreciation of our net worth. You don't find your net worth on a financial statement; you find it inside of you. Just look for it. And then, as you're looking, leap into the fire of God!

Yes, I said you should leap into the fire of God! The Bible tells us that "our God is a consuming fire."[15] God will consume the bad habits of our not-self with his consuming fire, if we ask him to. And having been delivered of our bad habits, we can express more and more of our Christ consciousness.

If we let the fire of God cleanse us a little bit every day, then one day we will be able to make that giant leap into the fire of God—just as Shadrach, Meshach and Abednego did. You will remember that King Nebuchadnezzar had these three Jews cast into a fiery furnace because they refused to worship "the golden image" that the king had set up. To his astonishment Nebuchadnezzar saw them walking in the midst of the fire along with a fourth man who was "like the Son of God."

When the king called the three men out of the fire, the officials gathered with him saw that not a hair of their heads had been singed nor their coats scorched, and there was no smell of fire upon them. So the king exclaimed, "Blessed be the God of Shadrach, Meshach and Abednego. He has sent his angel to rescue his servants who, putting their trust in him, defied the order of the king and preferred to forfeit their bodies rather than serve or worship any God but their own....There is no other God who can save like this." [16]

Now, most of us aren't ready to leap into the fire of God all at once, much less into a fiery furnace. I'm going to use the following analogy to illustrate my point. If you take this eyeglass case that I'm holding in my hand and move it toward a flame, any flame, eventually the case will melt.

Similarly, if God said to everyone here, "You come home right now—Daddy's calling," and you all started heading upwards trying to meet God, who is the ultimate consuming fire, your waxen wings would melt as Icarus's did and you would plunge headlong to the earth.

Do you know why your wings would melt? The answer is simple. It is because you have not fully absorbed the consciousness of God. You haven't wholeheartedly identified with God's consciousness because you haven't realized that God intended you to do just that: to fully incarnate his consciousness.

Furthermore, you haven't even begun to assess the heights and depths of his being as it fills all time and space and eternity. Once you fully identify with God's consciousness and his consciousness becomes your own, then you can become one with God without being destroyed by his all-consuming fire.

JESUS ISN'T THE ONLY CHRIST

We all have a sense of limitation. How do we get rid of that sense? We must first realize that God has a plan for us. His plan is in the Universal Christ, by whom all things were made. [17]

People confuse the Universal Christ with the identity of the man Jesus Christ. There is one Universal Christ. And that Universal Christ is individualized for each of us in the person of our Higher Self, our personal Holy Christ Self.

Jesus had the Christ in him, as we all do. But he was called "Jesus, the Christ" because he embodied the fullness of the Universal Christ. As the apostle Paul wrote of Jesus, "in him dwelleth all the fullness of the Godhead bodily."[18]

God didn't just create Jesus Christ and then turn around and make all the rest of us beggars. He created all the people on the planet for the same purpose—to become the Christ. Every one of you can become the Christ! God doesn't have a favorite son; we're all favorite sons. If it were not so, we would have very little hope for redemption.

If Christ had had his way, everybody on earth would have accepted him and his message a long time ago and hence graduated from earth's schoolroom. But instead, we see the same old Adamic doings that caused the expulsion from Eden: the old forbidden apple is still being passed and people are nibbling away at it just as they did then.

People are still doing the same things they've been doing throughout history. The crime sheets of the modern-day newspapers might as well be taken from ancient Rome or Pompeii. No matter what part of the world we look at, the same goings-on are plaguing the nations. Only today you've got a lot more people to multiply the world's negatives.

People get confused about the population problem. They don't understand that God assigned a certain number of souls to this planet. Out of those, a percentage are either in the astral plane or in the heaven-world awaiting rebirth. The remainder are in embodiment. People are dying and being reborn all the time. And there's no end to it until their souls attain union with God.

It reminds me of the little boy who looked under the bed and saw dust.

"Mama," he said, "You said we all came from dust and we're all going back to dust, right?"

"Right," said his mama.

"Well," he said, "somebody's either coming or going under the bed right now."

And that's the way it is. Somebody's either coming or going every minute.

The whole idea is this: take God very seriously, take your opportunity to be in embodiment very seriously, but don't take yourself too seriously. Learn to laugh at yourself. Learn to smile. Learn to be happy. Learn not to be overly conscious of your human personality.

When you hear footsteps in the night, ask, "Who goes there?" And the voice will reply, "God goes there."

Don't let God be a ship that passes in the night. Detain him. Ask him to tarry a while with you. You don't have to feel that God is remote. God is close—as close as your very breath.

THE BATTLE BETWEEN LIGHT AND DARKNESS WITHIN

Whatever you can accept of what I've said to you today is very important; what you cannot accept is not important.

Even if there's something I have said that you cannot accept, know that I have said it in the spirit of truth and because I know it to be true. Just because you may not know about something or have never proven it for yourself does not mean that it is not true.

Take the case of powered flight. The Wright brothers believed that their powered airplane, Kitty Hawk, would fly. But others did not believe in the power of mechanical flight until they saw it with their own eyes. You see what I mean.

In the churches today, many of the preachers, even the so-called great ones, stand up and preach a simple sermon for twenty minutes, pass the plate, sing a hymn and send the people home empty—or maybe they're left with a few platitudes.

What we teach is the greatness of God, and what we teach is great in his eyes because it is his very teaching. But in order to understand God's teaching, you first have to disabuse your mind of all illusions—the maya, the glamour, the karma.

You have to tear off your masks and put on the naked reality of your soul. And if you want Truth and you want Reality, you have to strip yourself of all the masks you've worn and strip yourself of this personality and that personality that you have donned in your past incarnations.

"Vanity of vanities; all is vanity," wrote Ecclesiastes. "I have seen all the works that are done under the sun; and, behold, all is vanity and vexation of spirit."[19]

You may not consider the masks that people put on to be maya, glamour and karma. You may not call them illusion. And maybe you say, "Well, they look very real to me."

But let me tell you something. There is much illusion and much fantasy in the world. There is much false idealism in the world. Many of today's college students are misguided by a false idealism and ultimately they are going to find ashes in the apple, ashes of nothingness. This is not a question of being young or old. Anyone can play host to illusion and fantasy.

I was looking at my son today—he's seven years old—and I said to myself, "Six years ago he was just an infant—how quickly those six years passed." How quickly the sands in the hourglass run out! We have infancy, childhood, the teenage years and young adulthood. Then we have maturity and old age. And so it goes, and it goes very fast.

So why should we have schisms within our own members—between body and soul, between mind and heart—or between ourselves and others? We are all children of the light, are we not?

You may say, "Well, there are children who are of the light and there are children who are not of the light." True. And there are people who have accepted the darkness into their worlds even as there are those who have rejected that darkness.

The apostle John wrote: "Light is come into the world, and men loved darkness rather than light, because their deeds were evil. For every one that doeth evil hateth the light, neither cometh to the light, lest his deeds should be reproved. But he that doeth truth cometh to the light, that his deeds may be made manifest that they are wrought in God."[20]

In reality darkness is not, for darkness is an absence of light. And darkness cannot remain when you allow the light of God to fill your world.

Yet things are not always black and white, are they? The life of a man is often gray because he is a mingling of self-ignorance and self-knowledge. When we adulterate our spiritual whiteness by mixing it with blackness, we get grayness.

We sometimes look for absolute perfection whether in ourselves or in others. It's there, but what colors it are the concepts we have about ourselves. When we look at ourselves, we tend to paint the lily pretty white. When we look at others, we tend to paint the lily not so white.

What is most important is that we nestle ourselves in the infinite care and consideration God extends to us. If you have the feeling that God doesn't care for you, get rid of it! God *does* care. But this is a two-way street. We have to care just as much about God as he cares about us. You see, sometimes we have to step up the stairs and step up our consciousness to get to the place where we really understand that God cares about us moment by moment.

I remember playing in the sandpile as a small child and building little sand castles while my father was digging a hole for a basement. I was thinking about the world from a level far above even my present-day understanding. I thought of a world that was meant to be—a world of perfection where people expressed love and kindness from their hearts. I envisioned this not as fantasy but as reality.

In my search I began to perceive, as I sought the kingdom

of heaven, that there was much more to the Holy Spirit than people had realized. It was like the experience of Siddhartha when for the first time he saw an old man, a diseased man, a corpse and a monk. It was then that the future Buddha realized there was old age, sickness and death in the world—and that the solution to human suffering could only be found through a spiritual path.

So I began to understand that the world was a spiritual as well as a material schoolroom. I saw that we had a lot to learn and that under the tutelage of the Great Ones we could excel in consciousness "from glory to glory."[21] Then, as time passed and I grew a little older, I began to realize that the condition of the world was worsening.

Robert Browning said, "God's in his heaven—All's right with the world."[22] Well, I know it's true that God is in his heaven, but I also know that all is not right with the world. Still, we cannot use as an excuse the fact that the world is not right. We have to make ourselves right regardless of the state of the world.

Let us make up our minds that we are going to do something for ourselves. And that something is to let go and let God do it. Let's let go of our tensions, our frustrations, our feelings that at any moment somebody's going to do us wrong. We have the abundant life and the abundant life is inside of us. It's there as surely as the lay of the land.

Whether it's in Texas or Oklahoma or Colorado, wherever it is in the world, *the land lies there.* Somebody has to plow it. Somebody has to till it. Somebody has to seed it. Somebody has to water it. And when the seed germinates and grows, it will bring forth abundant fruit.

Jesus said, "By their fruits ye shall know them."[23] But all do not have eyes to see the fruits. So be at peace and, above all, realize that no matter what turmoil may come upon this world, the most important battleground is, as Krishna said to Arjuna, within you.[24]

The light and the darkness struggle within our hearts for recognition. "How can the darkness, which doesn't exist, struggle with the light, which does exist?" you ask. Well, the light becomes darkness if we misuse it—that is, if we misqualify it. When we misqualify the light God gives us, it becomes darkness.

Jesus talked about this. He said, "The light of the body is the eye. If therefore thine eye be single, thy whole body shall be full of light." Think of it! If your eye is single—if you are devoted first and foremost to God—you will be filled with light. "But," Jesus said, "if thine eye be evil, thy whole body shall be full of darkness. If therefore the light that is in thee be darkness, how great is that darkness!"[25]

So remember: how you qualify or misqualify the light you have—which is God's energy—determines whether you will be filled with light or with darkness.

Getting back to the subject of the forgiveness of sins, I realize that what I have said is startling to those who have always thought that the doctrine of the forgiveness of sins means they don't have to make restitution for their wrongs, even if both God and man have forgiven them.

"Oh, it's so wonderful to be forgiven!" people say. Rasputin, that vile Russian "monk" who seduced hundreds of gullible women across Russia at the time of Czar Nicholas II by convincing them that they had to sin in order to be saved, used to say, "It feels so good to sin. And no matter how many times you sin, you can always go to confession, say you're sorry and be forgiven."

Let us not have the sense that we can beat the Great Law. Let us understand that our strength is not merely in religion or in the sense of being a member of a church. Our strength is in becoming one with God. And this is possible for us all.

ॐ

How to Develop the Christ Consciousness

❧ "A voice came from God to Moses,...
'I regard not the outside and the words,
I regard the inside and the state of the
    heart.
I look at the heart if it be humble,...
How long wilt thou dwell on words and
    superficialities?
A burning heart is what I want; consort
    with burning!
Kindle in thy heart the flame of love.'"

—RUMI

How to Develop the Christ Consciousness

Before we consider how to develop the Christ consciousness, we must create definitions that we can all understand. We need common denominators.

Let's begin by determining what consciousness is. Now, I may have my definition of consciousness and you may have yours, but I prefer to stay with the simple. As I see it, consciousness is an ever-flowing stream of intelligence that possesses an awareness of its environment and an awareness that may go far beyond its environment.

Consciousness is awareness, starting with the self. It is a state of being aware that you are you. And then you become aware of other people as distinct from yourself.

Our conscious awareness also possesses the capacity to deal with subtleties and innuendo. We don't even have to stop and consider whether someone is being superficial or sincere.

We already know through the spiritual faculties that are within us.

Our capacity to deal with human subtleties has come to be an innate art, one that even children learn at an early age. An infant may not be capable of speaking his mother tongue. Nevertheless he is able to deal in images that make it possible for him to identify his mother, his feeding time, his various needs, et cetera.

We go through many stages, from babyhood to childhood, the teenage years, adulthood and retirement. These stages don't have abrupt break-off points like stair steps.

You've probably heard the story about the young man who said that when he was sixteen he thought he knew a great deal more than his father knew. He felt his father really knew very little. When he turned twenty-one he said he was amazed at how much his father had learned in five years. So one stage of consciousness blends with the next.

All of this is dealing with the mundane. We are talking about consciousness in its lower ramifications. But we must deal with the realities of the mundane, of the earthy, before we can deal with heavenly realities.

CHRIST CONSCIOUSNESS IS A NATURAL PHENOMENON

What is Christ consciousness? It is the conscious awareness of the self as the Christ. When you attain the level of consciousness that Jesus Christ attained, you too will have the Christ consciousness.

There are, of course, various stages of Christ consciousness, and we can reach those stages gradually or very quickly. Some people seem to be born with Christ consciousness or it begins to manifest at an early age. Others work at it for a year or two and suddenly it manifests. Some work at it for ten years before it comes. Some take twenty years. Others work at it all their lives and then burst through to it just before they take their leave of this world.

Unfortunately, many people trick themselves. They have an idea that the development of the spiritual faculties leading to Christ consciousness is a breakaway from the natural phenomena of life. This is not so, and to think so is to be tricked by the forces of deceit and by those who would deliberately confuse the issues—turning light into darkness and darkness into light.

These forces try to make people think that the world is so complicated that they just can't cope with the fast pace of life. In some cases, this dilemma stimulates people to pursue the deeper mysteries of life and they find solace in the God within. Others may vegetate and do nothing except what is absolutely necessary to survive. Or they may rebel against the confusions of life by becoming nonconformists.

These are the miasmas of life. But Christ consciousness is not so. With Christ consciousness, we deal with naked reality or, as I prefer to call it, crystal-clear Christ clarity.

CHRIST CONSCIOUSNESS IS NOT DEVELOPED THROUGH OUTER THINGS

The apostle Paul revealed a formula that is truly wonderful. He said that we must put off the old man of the flesh and put on the new man of the Spirit.[1] Some spiritual seekers take this to mean that all of our mundaneness and humanness must be put away. When, in their own opinion, they have "put off the old man," they begin to criticize their brothers and sisters on the spiritual path.

We must be extremely careful that in our desire to develop the Christ consciousness we do not criticize, condemn and judge others. For criticism repels Christ consciousness. And when we criticize, we incur karma that we must one day tediously undo.

People have a tendency to fool themselves. They think they have received Christ consciousness simply because they have put away some of the things of this world. Maybe they don't smoke much anymore and they don't have quite as many highballs (or maybe they don't smoke or drink at all) and they've given up this and they've given up that.

They seem to feel that Christ consciousness is developed by giving up certain things the world does and that when one gives up these things Christ consciousness should automatically rush in.

Here is an enigma. I am referring to George Gurdjieff, who wrote *Beelzebub's Tales to His Grandson* and other writings and founded an institute in Paris. Gurdjieff didn't give up his cigarettes or his vodka. And from the standpoint of some seekers of God, these habits made Gurdjieff unacceptable as a spiritual teacher. Yet he was quite well-known as a mystic, and he was the teacher and guru of that great Russian writer Ouspensky, who wrote the *Tertium Organum.*

Somehow we get the idea that everyone who abstains

from this and that is just a little bit better than those who indulge. Once again I go to the apostle Paul, who speaks about this when he takes up the subject of eating meat. Eating meat poses a problem for many people because they think that it will prevent them from having Christ consciousness. "Meat commendeth us not to God," Paul said. "For neither if we eat are we the better; neither if we eat not are we the worse."[2]

Abstinence—not eating meat, for example—and being good little children in every way according to human standards does not guarantee us Christ consciousness. Conversely, just because you eat meat doesn't mean that you don't have Christ consciousness. I know people on both sides of the fence.

Christ consciousness is not guaranteed to you by what you *don't* do. It's more by what you *do* than by what you don't do. That's why George Gurdjieff, in spite of his drinking vodka and smoking cigarettes, was able to develop a certain state of consciousness that was above the ordinary. All the same, I happen to believe that he would have been better off without the vodka and the cigarettes.

It doesn't pay to judge people superficially. It doesn't pay to judge people at all. For Christ consciousness is not developed through outer things, whether by indulging in them or by abstaining from them. And the absence or presence of certain idiosyncrasies does not determine whether we are capable of rising to the level of Christ consciousness. As Paul asked, "O foolish Galatians, who hath bewitched you?... Having begun in the Spirit, are ye now made perfect by the flesh?"[3]

Now, it's very important that you do not hinder yourself

spiritually. A moment ago, I was straining to pull an idea out of my subconscious; and the harder I strained, the more I created a mental block, which prevented that thought from coming through at the exact moment I wanted it. We all have similar problems, and we have to learn to turn every defeat into a victory.

Our inherent divine intelligence

If we are going to develop Christ consciousness, we must first remove our blocks—our human blocks that make us block-heads. That's what we really are when we try to rely on hu-man reasoning and human intelligence alone—blockheads.

Actually, the great minds of our time are very much dependent on the divine intelligence within. They use divine intelligence all the time. The only thing is, they don't always acknowledge it.

Suppose that the blessed body elemental, whom they seldom acknowledge, failed to play its role in maintaining the balance of the body chemistry that allows God's energy to flow across the brain in its normal pattern. All of the chem-ical reactions they take for granted do not happen by acci-dent. They function through the divine intelligence. The body and all of its systems, the autonomic nervous system and so forth, function by God's grace.

Of course, the materialist does not believe this to be true. He seems to consider that all the parts of this little watch that he is, the mainspring (the heart) and all the coils and gears and wheels and wires and whatnot, work together independent of the divine intelligence. The materialist must think that all the parts we are made up of were taken up in an airplane and then dropped to the ground. On the way down the parts put themselves together, and when they got down here we had a nice twenty-one-jewel Swiss watch.

The materialist thinks that it all takes place automatically—that the watch has its own inherent intelligence. In fact, some materialists seem to feel that matter created itself. Today, many scientists are wedded to this idea. The grandfather of one of our staff members maintains that the world was created by happenstance, that everything is based on human intelligence and that man is his own creator.

Well, spiritually speaking, it actually happens to be true that we are our own creator, but we don't always know how to put all these things into focus. If you look through a telescope sometime and you start moving the knob back and forth, you will throw the telescope out of focus. There's only one little spot where it's in focus.

So it's not enough just to have ideas; we have to be able to focus them and apply them. It's not enough to have the idea, for example, that you should say your prayers at night. It's the doing that counts.

There is a great deal more to this universe than we—and I mean all of us, including the scientists—have ever stopped to think about. Sometimes when we pick up a new book, we are absolutely smitten with the idea that this book is tops—until we read the next one.

It reminds me very much of the salesman who was selling washing machines. The lady he was selling to had her doubts because she'd been stung before. She said, "I want to know that this washing machine will do everything I want it to do. I want the best washing machine in the world."

The man looked at her and he said, "Well, madam, I'm very sorry. I can only sell you the second-best washing machine in the world."

"That's not good enough for me," she snapped back at him. "I want the best."

"It hasn't been made yet," he replied.

That's the whole idea when we consider life from the standpoint of transcendence. Life has something more to offer us every day, because life is always upgrading itself.

Now, there's a difference between the words *trance* and *transcendence*. A trance is a state of partly suspended animation or a state of profound absorption or deep hypnosis. Afterwards you don't remember anything. You might say it is a suspension of consciousness. And where are you? Only God knows. But in transcendence, you know right where you are.

YOUR THOUGHTS MAY BE YOUR BROTHER'S STUMBLING BLOCK

As I said, the most important thing of all is to get rid of our human blocks. Don't judge people, because that's a diversion that will take you away from the source of Christ consciousness. If I start trying to figure out what everybody is about, I'm going to stop myself right in my tracks because my attention isn't on the Presence of God. It isn't on the laws of God. My attention is on a human being, who may be stumbling or who may be transcending.

We have to remember that people are rising in consciousness all the time. If your thoughts about them are not good and you decide they don't have Christ consciousness because of something they are doing, you are putting a stumbling block in their pathway.[4]

Your thoughts have wings. They fly to the person you are thinking about and they lodge in his desire body. At a certain point, when the human smog level gets dense and your negative thoughts begin to accumulate in that person's world, your little thought may be the straw that breaks the camel's back of his desire to do right. You may be to blame for his defeat because you put the stumbling block in his pathway.

So, it is always best to withhold judgment. That doesn't mean, however, that you shouldn't exercise your powers of discrimination. Discrimination is a quality of the Christ and a quality of Christ consciousness.

Discrimination is like a rudder. You'd be an awfully poor sailor if you were sailing without a rudder, because you need to have a rudder to steer. Likewise, you have to be able to discriminate good from evil in people if you're going to steer through the seas of life. You also have to learn how to walk the razor's edge between discrimination, which is able to divide the real from the unreal, and criticism, condemnation and judgment, which is harmful.

TURNING WITHIN AND LETTING GO

Let's get on now with some of the methods of developing Christ consciousness. First, you cannot develop Christ consciousness if your mind is involved in human affairs 100 percent of the time. You must make time for meditation. You must make time for reflection. You must make time for your soul to commune with God. You must make time to study and assimilate the Ascended Masters' ideas. You must make time to nourish the infant Christ-man that is within you.

The Christ-man manifests in the threefold flame within the secret chamber of your heart. The threefold flame is your divine spark. It's the eternal flame of God that sustains your lifestream as long as you are in embodiment. It's the torch of everlasting life that God gave you when he created you.

The threefold flame is made up of three plumes. As you face the Chart of Your Divine Self, the love plume is to your left, the wisdom plume is in the center, and the power plume is to your right (see pages 92 and 95).

The nature of the threefold flame is all positive. But that positivity is not supposed to stand still. You are not meant to leave the threefold flame as the babe in the crèche and sing once a year at Christmas "Gesù Bambino." God did not intend for that infant Messiah within you to remain an infant. You need to nurture him so that he will reach divine manhood.

The Christ always develops from within and never from without; yet outer experiences are what drive us within. There is a dearth of truth in our age because people are always turning without to solve their problems. And they keep turning without. They turn everything inside out and upside down. And, quite naturally, things do not work out as God intended.

I cite as an example the rebellion among some of today's youth. Look at the counterculture. It is full of young people who find fault with the dominant culture—often with good reason. They say society is "plastic," that it lacks heart and soul. They say it is unfair and unjust, especially to blacks. They are concerned about civil rights. They are concerned about the war in Vietnam. They are concerned about corrupt leadership.

As a result, some of our young people have become hippies or revolutionaries or acid heads. But there has been a cost. People trying to get high on drugs are missing the opportunity to attain the Christ consciousness, which would really get them high. And the sexual revolution is going to cause a lot of problems that we can't even anticipate today.

Then there are those who eat themselves to death or drink themselves to death or work themselves to death. I learned, for instance, that a corporation headquartered in Wilmington, Delaware, was losing as many as 20 percent of their top-flight executives to heart attacks, strokes and other serious conditions. These men were between fifty-five and sixty-five.

So the corporation bought a yacht. They anchored it on the Delaware River and arranged parties for the families of their employees so they could relax, because the mounting tensions were tearing them apart.

These are some of the problems of our time. The maelstrom of problems like these occupy about 90 percent of our attention during our waking hours. And about 10 percent of our time is involved in some form of fun, although sometimes the fun turns out to be a little more taxing than the daily grind.

Cutting down mental baggage

In order to develop the Christ consciousness, we have to let go of the world for certain stated periods. Jesus himself went up into a mountain to pray.[5] This signified his coming apart from the world. Jesus got on a boat, probably a stinky old fishing boat. (Most of them are, you know.) And he and his disciples launched out onto the Sea of Galilee. They got away from the shoreline, away from the people, and there they communed with God.

They didn't carry much in their suitcases, like some of our women do. But the men are even worse! The first time we went to California, we took up just about one whole compartment of the train. We had boxes and suitcases piled clear to the ceiling. I had microscopes and telescopes and heaven only knows what. I even had a radio transmitter along with me so I could broadcast. I was going to talk back and forth to my wife and others from my hotel room or anywhere in the city.

Oh, we had everything. We had so many porters when we went up to the hotel that they probably thought I was the Shah of Iran. I remember one time when I walked into the Dodge House in Washington, D.C., wearing my purple robe, and the elevator man looked at me and asked, "Are you a king or somethin'?" So we've really had a time learning what to take and what not to take with us. Well, I'm cutting it down now.

If you want to develop Christ consciousness, you have to cut down some of your excess baggage—your mental baggage. You have to get rid of your fears, whether of living or dying. In fact, you're not going to die. You're just going to step up or step down on Jacob's ladder.

Sometime, somewhere, though, we have to develop Christ consciousness. It has to come, or else we're not going to live.

That sounds enigmatic. First I say you won't die, and then I say you're not going to live. I'm going to tell you what the Lord told me. Jesus said that the passage in Exodus that says "No man can look upon the face of God and live"[6] means that no man can look upon the face of God and live *as man*.

When you have seen the face of God, you don't live as man anymore—you live as God. It changes you. The encounter with God turns you around 180 degrees. People don't have to know that you have changed. But you will know it, and that's all that is necessary. It's strictly between you and God.

So, you have to learn to go into your closet to pray.[7] You have to shut out the world. You have to see to it that no one else but you and God are in there. In these moments of communion with God, you have to shut out all the distressing states of consciousness that you have harbored and not let go of.

I sometimes think we have spent more time in the swamp than we have on the mountaintop. Most of us will agree on that. The question is, Why do we do it? The answer is mimicry.

We humans are better mimics than monkeys. We sit around and look at people and then we imitate what they do.

Often our vision is not centered on our God Presence and on the Ascended Masters, even those of us who have known them for decades.

What is producing great changes in our members is the opportunity to attend a service once a week. Think of it! Once a week people come here or go to our other centers. They experience a decree session, they hear a dictation and they are blessed by the Masters as they imbibe the light the Masters release.

NURTURING AN INTIMATE RELATIONSHIP WITH YOUR INNER CHRIST

If we could only give a little more of our time to developing Christ consciousness in ourselves and in others! It is a matter of investment. We need to start by investing a little something and then multiplying it.

Say a young man learns to play the stock market. He takes the money that he earned from his newspaper route and puts it into the market. And, lo and behold, he's doubled his money. Then his stock splits and within a short time his stock becomes worth even more. By the time he's ready to go to college, he's earned his tuition through stocks.

Well, how did he do it? First he had to invest his money and then he had to have faith that he would receive a return on his investment.

You have to put money in the bank if you expect to take it out. I've never seen any bank yet that will let you take it out unless you first put it in. And most banks today give you back a little bit more than what you put in.

You can invest in your own Christ consciousness by starting with what you have—your own God-given faculties. You can experiment with all the formulas you want to experiment with, but the whole idea is to use your five senses spiritually—your faculties of seeing, smelling, tasting, hearing and feeling—and to start looking toward God.

Now, the first thing that's going to happen to you when you do this is that you will suddenly realize that you can't visualize the face of God. You can only visualize the face of God if you have seen God. And you can only visualize the face of Jesus if you have seen him. And even when those who have seen Jesus try to sketch or paint his face, they come up short of the real Jesus.

Sallman and Hofmann and Hunt and other artists have all depicted Christ. Some people say, "Oh, I love the Sallman portrait." Others say, "I love Hunt." Others say, "Oh, I don't like that. I like Hofmann. He's more mystical."

Well, when it comes to defining the face of God or defining the face of Christ, it is based on individual perception. If we were all artists and we all painted our perception of Christ, each canvas would be different.

When it comes to developing the Christ consciousness, we are all nurturing our own *individualized* Christ-manifestation. If you want to sustain the Christ consciousness hour by hour, day by day, you have to enter into your own intimate relationship with your own inner Christ. You have to have a secure one-on-one relationship with the Christ.

In order for this to happen, you need to distance yourself from the notion that you are developing something that is stable in the universe, because from the standpoint of the human consciousness you are not. Humanity as a whole is incapable of stabilizing itself in the Christ consciousness. It is only going to be stable in you, you and you because person by person and individual by individual you have determined to make it so.

So, all of these depictions of Christ by famous artists are fine. They help us visualize Christ. All art that is inspired from above should be captured by the mind to help us develop the Christ consciousness within.

Why do you suppose we have created the Chart of Your Divine Self? Who could paint God? Who could even paint man as he really is? The Chart is an assist to understanding God. Beautiful music is an assist. Prayer and contemplation are an assist.

HELPING OTHERS DEVELOP THE CHRIST CONSCIOUSNESS BY PRAISING NOBLE EFFORT

Now, they may not know it, but all people need the Christ consciousness. And one way of developing the Christ consciousness in yourself is to help others develop what you yourself have not yet developed.

How do you like that? If you haven't developed the Christ consciousness in its fullness yourself, don't let that deter you from trying to help others develop it. You help others by being upbeat and by taking time to understand them and their problems.

A little while ago we talked about not criticizing others. Well, how about a little praise for others' efforts?

If you say, "Well, so-and-so hasn't tried very hard.

I mean, I saw him do something that wasn't right not too long ago," you're on the negative side. We don't want that. We are going to throw that out.

Did you ever consider what praise does for a little child? You go up to a child and you praise a drawing he made. It's crude but you say, "Oh, Johnny! What a beautiful picture you've drawn."

You're a parent or a teacher or a friend of this child. You are not necessarily praising the end result but you are praising his effort—an effort that at its own level was designed by the child to create something wonderful.

That is exactly what you have to learn to do to develop Christ consciousness in others as well as in yourself: recognize and praise noble effort. Don't try to classify someone's effort. Don't try to belittle it.

On the other hand, don't try to judge another's effort and say, "Well, this man is just a step away from his tenth initiation into the great zooma, zooma, zooma." In other words, don't decide that somebody is at this or that level of initiation or that, even though you are down here in the outer court, you are capable of judging the great beings that have climbed so far up the spiritual ladder of life that they are out of sight.

People analyze other people all the time. Every once in a while someone who has attended one of our meetings and has heard an Ascended Master give a dictation through me or Elizabeth says, "Well, that Master didn't know the past participle of that verb. If he were a Master, he would have known it."

In my early days as a Messenger, a man in Washington, D.C., was critical of me because when Saint Germain dictated through me I pronounced *fleur-de-lis* incorrectly. The correct pronunciation is "fleur-de-lees," not "fleur-de-lay."

Now, all my life I had pronounced it the wrong way. It wouldn't matter if Saint Germain or God Almighty spoke through me; unless he would have written *fleur-de-lis* out phonetically for me to practice ahead of time, I would have mispronounced it. And there isn't time for the Master to write it out phonetically because the dictation comes so fast. So the Masters have to use the idiom of the prophet.

Paul brought this out when he said, "The spirits of the prophets are subject to the prophets."[8] Truly, the Holy Spirit moves upon the consciousness of the prophet. But if a Messenger says "ain't" or "'tisn't"—which we don't usually hear from a Master—or if he goes off the beaten path of the vernacular, it isn't the fault of the Master, who certainly knows better. It simply means that the thoughtform of the word that came into the Messenger's consciousness from the Master's level was misinterpreted in the English language.

So, this man in Washington, D.C., had been chasing me all over town so he could get acquainted with me. He invited me out to dinner. He called me on my car telephone. He thought the sun rose and set in me. He was really friendly.

Then he came to one of our meetings and heard that mispronounced *fleur-de-lis*. Afterwards, when we were eating, he wouldn't sit by me. He moved across the room. I walked over and asked him what was the matter, and he said to me, "I'll have you know that you are a false prophet."

I said, "Oh? Why do you say that?"

"The French language has been spoken for centuries and it has always been spoken correctly," he said. "Saint Germain has spoken French correctly for several hundred years or more. I'll have you know that I have listened to mediums all over this country who speak perfect Chinese even though they don't consciously know a word of Chinese. You are a false prophet."

How silly people can get! They're willing to judge a book by its cover or even by its first chapter! I wouldn't dare to judge myself on that basis. I myself don't even know the beginning or the ending of my life cycles. It wouldn't be any fun if we knew the end from the beginning. It would be like going to an old movie that we had seen at least twenty-five times.

We have to get out of the habit of judging people. We need to be too busy attuning with the Christ to judge others. Think as Jesus Christ would think. Make up your mind to come apart from the world, as he did after the beheading of John the Baptist, when he departed by boat into "a desert place apart."[9] But be sure to put on a defensive armour[10] against those who would derail you the moment you start.

Now, this is a very important point. The minute you start to come apart unto God, the world will hate you, as it hated Jesus.[11] You can expect it. But you don't have to amplify the world's hatred of you by letting your expectations run away with you, which I've seen some people do. You can always invite problems. It's so easy to invite them.

The main thing is to help other people develop the Christ consciousness while you keep your armour on, while you set apart time for attunement with God, and while you forget the idea of drawing a portrait of Jesus Christ or of God.

Why did I say that? I said, "While you forget." I meant exactly that. Stop trying to define the Almighty. And watch out, because sooner or later someone is going to try to get you to box in the Christ consciousness. You had better not let that happen, because by boxing it into compartments of theology, the Christ consciousness will be lost.

START MEDITATING ON GOD AND DON'T GET CAUGHT UP IN THE PAST

I have tuned in—as Risë Stevens has[12] and as you may also have—to events that took place thousands of years ago. I have seen ancient scenes of past civilizations as if they were live on TV today. These scenes are all part of what we call the akashic records.

When you start to develop Christ consciousness, you must be careful not to get caught up meandering through the astral plane or in the akashic records. This may occur during states of reverie that sometimes accompany meditation. You start to meditate on God and the first thing you know, you're in a dreamy state. You may suddenly see before your mind the face of a girlfriend or some chum of yours.

The picture is there for a minute. It has no meaning. Then something else comes along. It's kind of a phantasmagoria, because it is nothing more than a haphazard playback from your subconscious memory. Letting reverie and imagination run away with you is a state of mind that is an enemy of your developing Christ consciousness.

All imagery from the past—latent, expressed, or otherwise—has to be set aside and consciousness has to be alerted. This is the truth and I have to state it. You have to get away from reverie and from sights and smells and sounds of the past in order to develop Christ consciousness, because you haven't had Christ consciousness before. What you have had is human consciousness.

If you're going to put off the old man or woman and put on the new, you have to create a frame of reference that at least resembles what you think the new man or woman should resemble. One of the ways to put off the old man or woman and develop Christ consciousness is to meditate on the Christ.

I visualize Jesus without too much facial definition. That's the way I started thinking about him several years ago. I mainly visualized the white robe and the radiance coming out of that robe. I didn't try to be too definite with it. I let the image develop on the film, so to speak. And I kept my attention on God, because God is higher than Christ. Christ comes out of the Source.

God is Spirit. Jesus said that those born of the Spirit are like the wind; it blows here and it blows there.[13] Nobody sees it. So when you visualize God, you don't really see God, but you see God's light as it emanates from the Christ.

After you have been doing this for a long time, you may experience an unusual happening. You may suddenly feel currents running all through your body, over your hands and down to your feet. You may feel an almost unspeakable joy. When this happens you know you are getting a wave of Christ's radiation.

As that wave passes through you, it aligns the inward parts of your being with the patterns of the Christ. Christ is putting his patterns into you at all levels—superconscious, conscious, subconscious and unconscious. And billions of cells—the building blocks of your memory body, your mind, your emotions and your physical body—become charged with Christ's radiance.

That's one of the ways you develop Christ consciousness. You further develop it through good deeds, through harmonious interchanges and through expressions of holy love.

Admitting your mistakes

You can't fool God and you can't fool man. And, in reality, you can't even fool yourself. You have to face the truth. You have to build solidly on the foundation of Christ all through life by simply asking yourself, "What would Jesus do in this situation?"

One time I stood in the lobby of a theater and a drunk came along and bought a big bag of popcorn. He had double butter put on it and then proceeded to dump the whole thing, popcorn and butter, all the way down the front of my nice suit.

Well, I didn't hit him, and I was reasonably self-contained. But I didn't behave quite the way I should have. I made him pay for dry cleaning the suit. He didn't offer to pay for it, and he got a little abusive with me. So I went ahead and made him pay for it. He didn't think I could, but I did. I took it as a human challenge, but I was wrong. That was several years ago. If I had it to do over again, I would just say, "Well, it was a mistake. God bless you."

That is what you have to do: admit your mistakes all the way down the line. If you're wrong, admit it. Now, people have the foolish idea that they should admit their mistakes to others. They think we should confess to our neighbors every mistake we make and then get down and kiss their boots.

If you feel that you have wronged someone to the point that it's causing them grief, you can go to them and say, "I'm genuinely sorry for what I did and I hope you'll forgive me." But you do not have to do this. I have done it and I would do it again if I felt it was necessary. Each circumstance breeds its own solution, and we must learn to accept that.

BUILDING FROM THE TEMPORARY REALITY OF THE PRESENT TO THE ETERNAL REALITY OF GOD

One mistake that people make as they try to develop the Christ consciousness is that they think they can separate out the tares from the wheat without destroying the wheat.[14] And they get discouraged because they don't see spirituality manifesting in themselves overnight.

Stop that foolishness! Today you are the sum total of all that you have been in the past. Your future will be the sum total of all that you have been in the past, too, and all that you will be. It's never too late to change. It's never too late to start over. It's never too late to correct your errors.

Today my consciousness recognizes that, in regard to the popcorn incident, perhaps I should have handled that a little differently. Yet even a Christ does not always behave in a manner that everyone might agree with.

Jesus went up to Jerusalem and found moneychangers in the temple and people selling oxen and sheep and doves. He made a whip out of small cords and drove them all out of the temple, and he kicked over the tables of the moneychangers. He gave them a good dressing down. That's what he did. And he said, "It is written, 'My house shall be called the house of prayer; but ye have made it a den of thieves.'"[15]

I have discussed this with Jesus. And he told me, "If I had it to do over, I would not have done it that way." That's absolutely true. He said, "How could I recommend this to my followers? How could I recommend that they go out today and try this? They'd be in jail, and I wouldn't want to have them put in jail."

But in the era in which he lived and under the circumstances that were going on in Jerusalem and considering his zeal, it was not out of character for him to so react. In the heat of the moment he could do this. The Bible says that after Jesus did this, "his disciples remembered that it was written, 'The zeal of thine house hath eaten me up.'"[16] But, you see, God didn't impute this to him. It didn't stop Jesus from being a Christ.

Even today some of the Christs who are on earth, and there are a few, don't always behave exactly as human beings think they should behave. But the Christs know that sometimes rash actions are the only way they will get results.

Sometimes, even by the Master's direction, I have dealt with people in an unusual way and they have learned something by it. And that's what the Master wanted. He wanted them to learn a lesson.

But you're not Jesus and you don't want to act the way he did because you don't have the attainment he had when he did it—even if in retrospect the Lord would have done otherwise. So don't try it, otherwise you might end up having to pay off a lot of karma. We want to cut our losses when it comes to our karma. We don't want to make any more karma if we can help it.

So we have to take the spiritual path by steps and stages. We first have to learn to jump over a twelve-foot hurdle without breaking an arm or a leg before we go to a twelve-and-a-half-foot hurdle. God will never hinder you or slow you down, but you can go too fast by pushing yourself without having the necessary support of moral standards and personal values to live by.

When you want to erect a building, you lay one brick on top of another and it's all tied to a foundation. But what do we have in America today? We have psychics and seekers after psychic phenomena all over the country who don't bother to put their bricks on foundations. They start with an airy nothingness, voices that mutter and peep,[17] and they mumble languages of demons and discarnates.

If you want to develop the Christ consciousness, you have to start with what you are and build on the fashion of things as they are. The way it works is this: You have a latticework on which your roses climb. The latticework represents the material consciousness. You have good and bad wood in the latticework. You have pure wood with good paint on it that's well-preserved and you have rotten wood.

What you have to do is let the rose of the soul climb

through this lattice. It keeps on climbing through the lattice, and the fragrance of the soul permeates everything. The roses come through the lattice, and then suddenly the light comes through. When it does, every bit of the rotten wood is cut out and is replaced, and the rest of the wood is changed. And you have what amounts to eternal substance, and the roses are growing on that.

You have to build from the temporary reality of the present to the eternal reality of God. If you can do this with no sense of struggle, recognizing your fellow pilgrims on the path and all humanity as travelers on the upward way no matter what their state of consciousness, you are going to become a Christ. But you're only going to become a Christ because your consciousness changes from a human consciousness into a Christ consciousness.

৯৫

Eternal Christmas in July

ॐ *"The real celebration of Christmas is the realization within ourselves of Christ Consciousness. It is of utmost importance to every man, whatever his religion, that he experience within himself this 'birth' of the universal Christ....In that land of everlasting Christmas...you will find Jesus, Krishna, the saints of all religions."*

—Paramahansa Yogananda

ॐ *"The important thing is not to think much but to love much; and so do that which best stirs you to love."*

—Teresa of Avila

CHAPTER THREE

Eternal Christmas in July

I've always believed that people are important, and I think this lecture, "Eternal Christmas in July," will show you just how important people really are.

I saw a skit once about a boy who was very unhappy with his sister and he didn't like his father. He thought he was being restricted. And so he asked that these people be x-ed out of his life. In fact, he wanted all people x-ed out.

One day, he woke up and he ran to see if his sister was there. She was lying in bed and he said, "X!" and she disappeared. He ran to the dog, but he didn't want to see the dog either. So he x-ed the dog out, and the dog disappeared. He made his father disappear and his mother disappear, and pretty soon he was alone in the world. He'd go down to the drugstore and make ice cream sodas for himself. He could do everything he wanted to. And this, of course, was all a dream.

After a while, tiny little tears began to stream out of his tear ducts "because," he said, "I don't have anybody to play with. There just isn't anybody around." He felt awfully bad about this. He was really glum.

So he got down on his knees and he prayed and he prayed and he prayed. Pretty soon his sister came back, then his dog came back. His father reappeared. Then his mother reappeared. One by one they all came back. And he just hugged everybody. He was very, very happy to see them.

The skit was quite well done. It effectively made the point that, in reality, we need people. Oh, maybe we don't like some of the things people do. I suppose that a lot of people could criticize us and we could criticize a lot of people if we wanted to. But I don't suspect that that would do much good, because people will do pretty much what they want to do when they're motivated by human will. When they're motivated by the divine will, of course, they try to align with the divine will. And we all ought to realize how very important the divine will is.

THE ADVENT OF THE CHRIST IN YOUR HEART

I selected this theme, "Eternal Christmas in July," to create in your consciousness the awareness that when we correctly understand the meaning of the "Christ Mass," we will see that every day, in effect, is Christmas.

Every day is Christmas because the advent of Christ that occurred two thousand years ago is a circumstance that exerts its influence every day throughout the year to produce that greatly desired commodity on this planet—peace on earth, goodwill toward men.

People must be important to God. If they were not important to God, he would not have created them to begin with, nor would he have exhibited so much love for them.

It says in the Bible, "For God so loved the world that he gave his only begotten Son, that whosoever believeth in him should not perish but have everlasting life."[1] Do you understand the meaning of that? God so loved the world that from its foundation he gave his Son to us. For "all things were made by him; and without him was not any thing made that was made."[2]

Now, whatever happens above, happens below. The patterns of the things that are in the heavens are mirrored within the realm of our heart. There is a dual activity, the activity of the macrocosmic clock and the activity of the microcosmic clock—as Above, so below.

In other words, the advent of the Christ was not just a one-time event. It is an event that we can actually mirror within our heart. In relation to this, the Master Jesus tells us, "They shall cry out and say, 'Christ is here' and 'Christ is there.'" "Go not after them," he says, "for, behold, the kingdom of God is *within you*."[3]

The kingdom of God is the consciousness of God. When you feel the reality of the kingdom of God, you find that it is a magnificent, cosmic common denominator that transcends all denominations, that transcends all the machinations of human opinions, that raises you until you can think like a Christ and stop thinking like a human.

If we were permitted to open the doors of this ashram to you or to the rank and file of the world to reveal the greatest of mysteries, I can assure you that many would feel self-chastened at their first wrong thought. The Masters do this. They make you sensitive to your every thought, word and deed.

Master Serapis Bey, whose retreat is at Luxor, Egypt, is a very stern disciplinarian. If you walk into one of his meetings while he is speaking and you entertain a single wrong thought, he will not hesitate to put you out on the spot. And not just for the day, but in some cases for the rest of your life.

This should tell you that as a rule the greatest Masters do not tolerate human conceit or deceit. Nor do they tolerate human criticism, human condemnation or human judgment.

They do not tolerate such states of mind in their disciples because such states put a damper on all divine or human action. They bring down the vibration of the individual or the group to the lowest level possible and are always the product of the carnal mind. So, in light of this almost universal human propensity, I want you to think with me today as you would imagine Christ would think.

GOD DOESN'T HAVE FAVORITES

Now, our first premise is taken from the words of Jesus "Inasmuch as ye have done it unto one of the least of these my brethren, ye have done it unto me."[4] This is one of the most noble thoughts you could possibly think because it will bring you to a different view of the men and women you meet wherever you are. You will see them as though they were the Christ.

Saint Peter, a Jew, had this experience. And it changed forever his view of the Gentiles. While Peter was staying in Joppa, he had a vision. He saw an amazing sheet descending from heaven. The sheet was filled with all manner of creatures, of four-footed beasts and creeping and crawling things. With the vision came these words, "Rise, Peter. Kill and eat."

Then came the answer of the apostle: "Not so, Lord." (Remember, he's talking to the Lord.) "Not so, Lord," he said. (He rejected the Lord's command.) "For I have never eaten anything that is common or unclean."

The voice spoke to him again and said, "What God hath cleansed, that call not thou common."

Peter was stuck in his old momentums, as many people are. It didn't matter that the Lord was speaking. He was Peter and he had his own ideas about things. He had great zeal in the Lord, he had great devotion to God and he was a good man.

But at that juncture, he was not quite good enough. For when the voice came a second time, "Rise, Peter. Kill and eat," Peter's answer was the same: "Not so, Lord." And the voice spoke again, "What God hath cleansed, that call not thou common."

This happened a third time and then the sheet ascended and the vision was withdrawn. The Lord was trying to teach Peter a lesson, and Peter was trying to figure out what it was.

The Holy Spirit then told Peter that three men were coming to see him and that he shouldn't hesitate to go with them. The men arrived and said that the centurion Cornelius, a devout Gentile, had asked them to bring Peter to his home.

They explained that an angel had directed Cornelius to send for Peter. In the meantime Cornelius, with his kinsmen and close friends, was waiting for the apostle to arrive.

What did Peter say when he met these Gentiles? He said something that was quite radical for his day, something that literally wiped away centuries of racial prejudice. He said: "Ye know how that it is an unlawful thing for a Jew to associate with or visit anyone of another nation; but God has shown me that I should not call any man common or unclean. . . . Of a truth I perceive that God is no respecter of persons; God doesn't have favorites. But in every nation, anyone who fears him and does what is right is acceptable to him."

Then Peter preached to the Gentiles who had gathered at the home of Cornelius. And the Holy Spirit came upon them and they all spoke with tongues. When Peter saw this, he realized that the Lord wanted the Gentiles to be baptized.[5] By allowing them to be baptized and by accepting them into the Christian community, Peter opened the doors to the spread of Christianity among the Gentiles.

The lesson that God gave to Peter was that he should not treat any person as common or unclean. This lesson is also conveyed in the story of the gentleman and the leper, which I have told in a number of my lectures. A gentleman is confronted by a leper and told by God to clasp the leper to his heart. The gentleman shudders and shakes and absolutely refuses.

The voice of God speaks to him again and again. Finally, the Spirit overpowers him and he realizes that he must bow to the will of God. He embraces the leper, the leper is transformed, and the gentleman is holding the living Christ.

HUMILITY IS THE BEST BEDFELLOW

We live in a world where practically all the struggle and strife and unhappiness—personal and collective—are the result of mankind's failures. Unfortunately, we find that some adherents of the world's religions place greater importance upon the avenging sword and the judgments of men than they place upon compassionately tolerating people's idiosyncrasies and manifesting the Christ consciousness.

The problems of the world lie in this and nothing else: men will not surrender the fruit of their own ego. They always qualify the great statement "I am" with "me." They say, "I am me, and therefore what I have judged to be so is so," and "This person is eating with sinners. This person is drinking with winebibbers."

They find little flaws in people, and they criticize and condemn. And in so doing, they lose the peace and happiness and joy that is to be found in universal brotherhood and in the spirit of compassion for others.

Whenever I think of these things, I also think of the statement "He who knows not and knows not that he knows not, he is a fool. Shun him. He who knows not and knows that he knows not, he is a child. Teach him. He who knows and knows that he knows, he is a wise man. Follow him."

From all the spiritual experiences I have had in this life, I have found that humility is the best bedfellow, the best friend. I recall very well that when I was a member of the Indian Society at the University of Wisconsin and I was holding meetings on spiritual teachings, a young Indian student would always come up to me after the meetings. He would offer his *pranam*[6] to me and invite me to his home, and he would always say, "Oh, we are so glad to see you, Mr. Prophet." Well, I thought very highly of him and his associates. I went to see them at least once a month and took tea with them.

One night I found myself sitting at the counter in a drugstore in Madison, Wisconsin, next to the president of the Indian Society. He turned to me and said, "Mr. Prophet, you are too fine a person to be taken in by these people."

I said, "What are you talking about?"

He said, "The people that you are calling on hate you."

I said, "What? Are you kidding?"

He said, "Not at all. They hate you with a passion and they wish to heaven you would evaporate or die. I have been struggling with whether or not to tell you."

"But," I said, "they're so nice to me."

He said, "This is Indian hypocrisy."

When Mrs. Prophet worked at the United Nations in New York, she encountered the same hypocrisy. In fact, many people carry this disease—the disease of hypocrisy. They will speak great words of respect to you to your face, but behind your back they will damn and criticize you.

You cannot criticize anyone without criticizing the Christ in that person. It is particularly unsavory when spiritually minded people, who are doing their level best within the framework of their understanding, come under the hammer of people's criticism.

This is the problem that continues to beset the Christian church today. And the Church has not solved it any more than we have solved it. Nor has the Great White Brotherhood.

THE INVERSION OF THE REALITIES OF GOD

I remember a story about God having a conference with Satan. The story is similar to Job's story. God finds a certain woman down here on earth who is doing a great job for him. She's helping people understand a little more about who and what God really is. So the Lord is boasting about her to Satan and he says, "Have you seen this daughter of mine down there and what a wonderful job she's doing?"

The devil snickers.

"Well, do you see what miracles she's accomplished?" God asks. And he tells Satan how she has been an angel to the poor and needy, how she has taken orphans into her own home and raised them, and most of all how she is breaking the bread of life and is teaching people the real meaning of Christianity.

"Yeah," says Satan, "that's right. I agree. She's doing a beautiful job. But just wait till she tries to get organized!"

So, when it comes to religion, everybody has their own ideas about how it should be done. And that's why it's so difficult to organize an activity of the Great White Brotherhood. Because, you see, there are about as many recipes for religion as there are for plain old country piecrust! People just can't agree on what's the best religion any more than they can agree on what's the best piecrust.

When we first started The Summit Lighthouse activity, I wore $19 suits. (And this is important. Your soul's salvation may depend on the fact that I wore $19 suits!) Today I wear $200 suits, and I'll tell you why. When I wore the $19 suits, everybody felt sorry for me, and so they were always giving me a donation.

But for over five years now, ever since I started wearing $200 suits, I haven't received a personal donation to speak of. This doesn't bother me at all because I didn't come into this work with money in mind. I never cared whether we were in a manger or in a mansion, as we are now.

Actually, it was the Master Saint Germain, together with the Master El Morya, who brought this piece of property to our attention through a realtor in Colorado Springs. They led us to it and then saw to it that the owners cut the price in half in answer to our prayer, enabling us to purchase it with a small down payment. And so La Tourelle (French for "turret" or "little tower"), as our home is called, has become the headquarters of The Summit Lighthouse in the United States.[7]

If you look up at the gutters on the corners of this beautiful four-story brick building, you will see Saint Germain's fleur-de-lis impressed upon the gutters. These fleur-de-lis were put there when the house was built—another sign that the Masters had kept the mansion for The Summit Lighthouse. And so the Masters have directed us to do everything we have done to expand our headquarters and our worldwide movement.

In the same seemingly miraculous way that Saint Germain secured La Tourelle with, you might say, the snap of his fingers, he can heal the flaws in diamonds or precipitate jewels. During the eighteenth and nineteenth centuries, as Saint Germain moved throughout the courts of Europe as "the Wonderman," he was known to remove the flaws in the jewels of the glitterati and the royalty. The Master can create a sea of cosmic fire around a flawed jewel, melt it into the molten state in the wink of an eye, and then bring it back as a perfected crystal.

On one occasion (this took place in Paris) Saint Germain was seated at a table with a gathering of guests who had come to be entertained and, in a more serious vein, to test his powers. Some among them were looking for phenomena while others questioned his adeptship. (I know this happened, even though I was not an eyewitness to the event.)

So, responding to their thoughts and their queries, the Master said, "Well, this won't pose any problem at all." Whereupon, Saint Germain stretched out his arm and the shutters flew open. The next thing anyone knew, the table and all of the chairs with the guests still seated on them were hanging above the sidewalks! No doubt they all hung their heads in shame.

As the Wonderman of Europe, Saint Germain would walk down the streets of Paris healing children and handing out jewels to the poor so that they could buy bread. Mothers who were raised in devout Catholic families grabbed their children as Saint Germain passed by to make sure that his shadow did not touch their children. The mothers called him *"le diable! le diable!"* as he passed by. They called him "the devil."

Down through the centuries, one of the conspiracies of the false hierarchy has been to attempt to invert the realities of God. The fallen angels and aliens have attempted to insert false ideas into people's consciousness. For instance, they have promoted the idea that the devil is involved in the activities of the Great White Brotherhood and in the practice of cosmic law as it functions on earth. They have also attempted to convince people that God is involved only in Christian churches, Buddhist temples, Hindu temples, Islamic mosques and so forth and that he does not abide in the cathedral of the heart.

We have to be very careful in our application of Jesus' axiom "By their fruits ye shall know them."[8] We must make sure that we ourselves know and understand that God is functioning through all who will drink freely of the water of life.[9] He's not particularly concerned with the cup you drink from—such as an old, battered tin cup like me—but with the water that you drink out of the cup, which is the water of eternal life. The cup is merely the conveyer of the water.

We must begin to depend on God

Why am I taking my time today to tell you this? Because Saint Paul said, "When I was a child, I spake as a child, I understood as a child, I thought as a child. But when I became a man, I put away childish things."[10]

In the advent of our own God star, in the radiance of our own natal star shining in our own sky, in the advent of our Christ birth—our birth into Christ reality with its ageless wisdom—it must happen sometime, somewhere that we discard our dependence on the human person and really begin to depend on God.

We can learn a lot about dependence on God from the

life of Saint Francis. Before he dedicated himself to God, Francis lived a carefree and worldly life. But when he became a true devotee of God, when something began to tug at his soul that changed him, there was no stone too heavy for him. He literally broke his body for God. Francis gave everything to God and depended on God for everything. And in turn, God gave himself fully to Francis.

Let's enter the world of Saint Francis for a moment so you can understand what I mean. He was born in 1181 or 1182 in the town of Assisi in Italy. His father was a well-to-do cloth merchant. Francesco di Pietro di Bernardone, as Francis was called then, had a certain worldliness and zest for life that made him a favorite among the young men of Assisi.

When he was about 20, he fought in a war and was a prisoner of war for a year. Later he set out to join soldiers who were fighting in southern Italy but had a dream telling him to return home. Once he was back in his hometown, he found that he didn't enjoy his old lifestyle of frolic and fun the way he used to. He turned more and more to prayer and contemplation.

One day he had an experience that changed forever the way he looked at the world around him. He met a leper, covered with sores. Just the sight of the man repulsed him. But instead of letting his aversion get the upper hand, he had a breakthrough. As he reached out to give the leper alms, Francis kissed him. From then on, Francis began to devote himself to serving the sick.

The next turning point in Francis' life came as he was praying at the broken-down church of San Damiano outside

Assisi. He heard a voice tell him, "Go, Francis, and repair my house, which as you see is falling into ruin." Now, Christ was calling him to save the Church, but Francis took the command literally. He walked the streets of Assisi begging for money to fix the church.

Some of the townspeople made fun of Francis. They laughed at the sight of the once-wealthy young man now dressed in a shabby tunic begging for money. But Francis didn't flinch an inch. He went on to rebuild the church of San Damiano as well as two other deserted chapels.

Francis awakened to his real mission when he heard a reading from the Book of Matthew during Mass one day. In the passage, Jesus was sending the apostles away to preach. Jesus told them to take "no gold, nor silver, nor money" with them.[11] At that moment, Francis realized that God was calling him to a life of poverty and preaching.

Even though he wasn't a priest, Francis became an ardent evangelist. He wooed the people of Assisi to the love of Christ. Those who heard his homilies were drawn closer to God, for Francis had that unique ability to touch a place deep inside the heart.

Francis soon attracted disciples. He wrote a simple rule of life for them and asked the pope to approve it. The pope's advisors warned him that the way of life Francis had outlined for his disciples was unsafe and impractical. But in a dream, the pope saw Francis holding up the Lateran basilica (the pope's church in Rome), which looked as if it were ready to collapse. So the pope decided to approve Francis' rule and gave him and his friars the commission to preach repentance.

A couple of years later, a young noblewoman of Assisi, Clare, begged Francis to allow her to become one of his followers. So Francis founded a second order for her and other women disciples, known as the order of the Poor Clares. He later established a third order, the Brothers and Sisters of Penance, for lay people who wanted to adopt the Franciscan way of life while living in the world.

Francis had a simple formula for saving mankind: the imitation of Christ and brotherly love. He taught his followers to obey the Gospel, to care for the suffering, to preach and to embrace poverty as their bride.

In the early days, he and his brothers helped lepers and others who suffered. They earned their food by working at a trade or at neighboring farms. If they had no work, they would beg for what they needed, but they would not accept money. In later years, Francis preached in central Italy and traveled to Egypt to try to convert the Saracens. He sent his friars in pairs to preach as far away as Spain, Germany and Hungary.

Well, the Franciscan orders grew rapidly. The men's order numbered over five thousand in Francis' own lifetime! This was a mixed blessing, though, because as the order grew bigger some Franciscans wanted to amend Francis' strict but simple lifestyle. They argued that it wasn't workable. But he always held firm to his original allegiance to Lady Poverty.

Among Francis' most winning qualities were his sincerity and humility. Once, after he had been very sick, he started a sermon by saying, "Dearly beloved, I have to confess to God and you that during this Lent I have eaten cakes made with lard." Francis paid special attention to the sick and poor. He would even stay with lepers and share meals with them from the same plate.

As you know, Saint Francis is often pictured surrounded by birds and other animals. That's because the animals were his friends. He saw the presence of God in nature and therefore had a great love and respect for all creatures. All created things, he said, are our brothers and sisters because we all have the same Father.

Another endearing quality of Saint Francis was that he loved to sing praises to God—and he sang them in the common language of the people rather than in Latin. One time while he was visiting Clare and the community of nuns near the end of his life, he composed his famous "Canticle of Brother Sun," which praised the Creator and his creation. And for a week he did nothing but sing it over and over again.

Two years before his death, Francis received the miracle of the stigmata—marks resembling the wounds of Jesus on his hands, feet and side. During the last two years of his life, he was almost totally blind and was in constant pain. He passed on at the age of forty-four or forty-five. Just two years later, the Church declared Francis to be a saint.

Saint Francis is one of the most beloved saints of all time. He celebrated life and swept everyone up in his simple, childlike nature. He was very human and very divine. His cheerfulness and love of life—the same qualities that had made him so popular as a young man in Assisi—were infectious.

Life with Francis was like celebrating Christmas every

day, because for him every day was an occasion to imitate Christ and to develop a little more of the Christ consciousness.

I will say it again because it bears repeating: When we pause to consider Christmas in July, we ought to also consider the advent of the Christ consciousness as penetrating the whole substance of the year and being interwoven in the tapestry of the days. And Christmas ought to be an everyday affair, and we ought to sing of "peace on earth, goodwill toward men."

AM I MY BROTHER'S KEEPER?

This happens to be one of *the* most important thoughts of God and of Christ himself—that men should be kind to one another and love one another. John wrote, "God is love.... If we love one another, God dwelleth in us and his love is perfected in us."[12]

John, like Saint Francis, had a big hang-up, to use the vernacular. He was hung up on the idea of love. To him it meant life.

In the Great White Brotherhood we have a saying, "Love, Light and Life." Unfortunately, this saying has been mocked by those who have no contact with the Brotherhood.

The most important thing you can do is to look for the God in people. If you find fault with your world, if you don't like the Liberty Bell because it has a crack in it, well, get in there and pitch! This is your universe. God gave you dominion over the earth because he wanted you to exercise your free will to help produce peace on earth, goodwill toward men.

The reason we don't have peace on earth right now is

that people aren't working at it. The bulk of those who control the planet are working to produce chaos. Tiamat, the female dragon,[13] shakes the earth and without purpose.

"Inasmuch as ye have done it unto one of the least of these my brethren, ye have done it unto me."

Am I my brother's keeper?

The question has been asked by many. Being your brother's keeper is what it's all about. This is what the ministry of Jesus Christ was all about. This is what the love and devotion and holy wisdom of Gautama Buddha was all about.

Jesus said: "This is my commandment, that ye love one another, as I have loved you. Greater love hath no man than this, that a man lay down his life for his friends."[14] This teaching is no different from the message of Gautama Buddha.

A disciple once asked Gautama: "Would it be true to say that a part of our training is for the development of love and compassion?" Gautama replied: "No, it would not be true to say this. It would be true to say that the *whole* of our training is for the development of love and compassion."[15]

Gautama's entire life was an expression of love, compassion and sacrifice for the sake of others. He was born of a noble family in northern India in the 6th century B.C., about five hundred years before Jesus. His father was very protective, and he did everything in his power to shelter his son from contact with pain or suffering. He surrounded him with every conceivable luxury. At sixteen, Gautama married. He loved his wife, but as he grew older he became restless and dissatisfied with his princely existence.

When he was twenty-nine, he saw four things that he had

never seen before, and they changed his life. During three trips outside the palace, he saw a decrepit old man, a man racked with disease and a corpse. For the first time in his life, he realized that there was suffering and death in the world. On a fourth trip he saw a monk, and this inspired him to find the cause and the cure for human suffering.

So, in the middle of the night he left his wife, his newborn son and his palace to become a wandering ascetic. He studied with the most learned sages of his day and then joined a group of five ascetics to practice severe austerities. After six years of hardships, Gautama became so weak that he almost died. He realized that his excessive asceticism was not helping him to achieve his goal. So he decided to renounce his path of austerities and seek a path of enlightenment on his own.

One day a villager's daughter gave a strengthening meal of rich rice milk to Gautama. He then sat beneath a fig tree, vowing not to move until he'd gained enlightenment. But before he could attain enlightenment, he had to meet some challenges.

Mara, the Evil One, sent his three voluptuous daughters to seduce Gautama. Next Mara's armies assailed Gautama with hurricanes, a flood, flaming rocks, deadly weapons, demons and total darkness. Finally, the evil Mara challenged Gautama's right to be doing what he was doing. He demanded that Gautama get up and leave because, he said, Gautama was sitting in his seat!

None of these assaults or temptations moved the Buddha-to-be. He tapped the earth and the earth thundered: "I bear you witness!" Mara promptly fled.

After that Gautama entered into a deep meditation and at last attained enlightenment. He had become a Buddha, which means an "awakened one." But he did not remain in that blissful state. Out of compassion for his fellowmen, he once again turned his attention to the world.

He traveled to the city of Benares and delivered his first sermon to the five ascetics who had been his former companions. They became the first monks of his *Sangha,* which means "Community." Gautama spent the rest of his life as a traveling missionary, preaching for forty-five years.

The message Gautama taught in his first sermon is still the cornerstone of Buddhism today: the Four Noble Truths and the Eightfold Path. The Four Noble Truths are (1) that life is *dukkha,* "suffering"; (2) that the cause of this suffering is *tanha,* "desire" or "craving"; (3) that suffering will cease when the craving that causes it is forsaken and overcome; (4) that the way to this liberation is through living the Noble Eightfold Path.

The Eightfold Path is also called the Middle Way. Gautama advocated the Middle Way because he'd learned from his own experience that the two extremes of sensual indulgence and harsh asceticism don't lead to liberation.

You can look at the Eightfold Path as eight practical ways to walk the Middle Way and attain spiritual liberation. This path consists of right understanding or views, right thought or aspiration, right speech, right action or conduct, right livelihood, right effort, right mindfulness, and right concentration or absorption.

ᴿEINCARNATION:
THE DOCTRINE OF DIVINE FAIRNESS

As you know, the concept of reincarnation is important in Buddhism. Gautama taught: "What we are today comes from our thoughts of yesterday, and our present thoughts build our life of tomorrow."[16]

But one fact you may have overlooked is that the concept of reincarnation was taught by the Master Jesus. Reincarnation allows us the opportunity to fully realize the kingdom of God—that is, the consciousness of God—within. For the law of reincarnation states that your soul must reincarnate again and again until you attain immortal life through union with God.

Because of my great respect for my beautiful mother, for many years I wouldn't allow myself to believe in reincarnation. I wouldn't have believed in it even if I had died, come back as a baby and remembered that I had lived before. I would have been sure that it was the doctrine of Satan, because that's what my mother had taught me.

But reincarnation wasn't and isn't a doctrine of Satan. It is the doctrine of divine fairness. It is God's way of equalizing life's opportunities for all. The doctrine of reincarnation was a part of the belief of some Christians in the early Church. It was taught by Saint Francis in the public squares. Yet it is still not a part of Christian doctrine.

Why? In large part because of the sixth-century Byzantine rulers Justinian and Theodora. Both of them had a habit of meddling with Christian theology. Theodora even caused the demise of the pope.

Justinian dealt a death blow to Christian belief in reincarnation when he convened the Fifth Ecumenical Council of the Church, which anathematized (cursed) the teachings of the eminent theologian Origen of Alexandria on the preexistence of souls. For if there is no such thing as preexistence, then there can be no such thing as reincarnation.

So from that time on, Christians were considered heretics if they believed in reincarnation. And Justinian and Theodora did everything in their power to see to it that any teaching on reincarnation was removed from the Bible.

Why were Justinian and Theodora set against the doctrine of reincarnation? Well, Theodora had been a prostitute before she married the emperor Justinian. Having risen from courtesan to empress, she couldn't conceive of coming back in another life as a prostitute or someone who would have to serve others. So, as Noel Langley writes in his book about Edgar Cayce and reincarnation, Theodora and Justinian were intent on removing from the Bible the references to reincarnation.[17]

Let's go to the verse of scripture that was overlooked when the references to reincarnation were removed. This verse will show you the doctrine of reincarnation as clear as day. It involves the interesting life of John the Baptist, who was the reincarnation of the prophet Elijah.

Before Elijah was taken up into heaven, he was walking with his disciple Elisha, who was later embodied as Christ Jesus. As Elijah was preparing to be caught up into heaven in a chariot of fire, he turned to Elisha and asked him what he wanted.

"Ask what I shall do for thee before I be taken away from thee," Elijah said.

Elisha replied, "Let a double portion of thy spirit be upon me."

Elijah turned to his disciple and said, "If thou see me when I am taken from thee, it shall be so."

Then Elijah ascended into heaven in a chariot of fire. The fire element conveyed his body into the cosmic cloud. His mantle fell from him and Elisha picked it up and smote the waters of the Jordan River. And the double portion of the spirit of Elijah rested upon him.[18]

In Elijah's final incarnation as John the Baptist, the prophet said of his former disciple, "He [Jesus] must increase, but I must decrease.... One mightier than I cometh, the latchet of whose shoes I am not worthy to unloose."[19] And earlier, when Jesus' mother, Mary, who was with child, approached Elisabeth, the mother of John the Baptist, the babe John leaped in Elisabeth's womb for joy. The babe recognized the mastery of God in "that holy thing" that would be born of Mary.[20]

Now, here's the key passage. As Peter, James and John were coming down the mountain with Jesus after having witnessed Jesus' transfiguration and the appearance of Moses and Elijah, they asked the Lord, "Why, then, say the scribes that Elijah must first come?"

Jesus turned to them and said, "Elijah has already come and they did not know him but did to him whatever they pleased." Then Matthew records that "the disciples understood that he spake unto them of John the Baptist."[21]

John, you see, was beheaded by Herod. John had been put in prison because he had rebuked Herod for his unlawful marriage to Herodias. Salome, the daughter of Herodias, danced before Herod, and he promised to give her whatever she asked for. Prompted by her mother, she asked for the head of John the Baptist on a platter.[22]

So, the Master Jesus revealed to his disciples that John the Baptist was the reincarnation of the prophet Elijah. And Jesus said that "among them that are born of women there hath not risen a greater than John the Baptist."[23]

Truly, John the Baptist was the greatest man ever to be born of woman. Like Jesus, Saint Germain and Mary, Elijah ascended to God. But the extraordinary difference between Elijah and almost all others who have made their ascension is that he is one of the very few who balanced 100 percent of their karma, made their ascension *and then reincarnated*.

Don't let anyone tell you that they made their ascension and then came back into a physical body again. This is not a common occurrence. It may happen once in 2,500 years or not at all.

Why did the Ascended Master Elijah return to the Galilean scene reincarnated as John the Baptist? To prepare the way for Jesus, who was the avatar of the Piscean age. John was the one spoken of by the prophet Isaiah as "the voice of one crying in the wilderness, 'Prepare ye the way of the Lord. Make his paths straight.'"[24]

The prophet Malachi concluded the Old Testament with a prophecy of the coming of Elijah: "Behold, I will send you Elijah the prophet before the coming of the great and dreadful day of the LORD. And he shall turn the heart of the fathers to the children, and the heart of the children to their fathers, lest I come and smite the earth with a curse."[25]

So by celebrating our "Eternal Christmas in July," we are able to delve into some of the Christ mysteries that span the centuries.

OUR SALVATION IS THROUGH FREE WILL AND THE MASTER WITHIN

We have to understand the great mystery that the Christ is the Christ of the ages. He was the Christ of the ages before his nativity and he will be the Christ of the ages forever. "Jesus Christ, the same yesterday and today and forever!"[26]

Whatever age you live in, the kingdom of God is within you. Ten generations from now, if you are a great-great-great-great-great-great-great-great-grandmother or -grandfather, you may find that you are your own great-grandma or your own great-grandpa. Or, if you've made your ascension, you may find that you are striving to remove from the consciousness of mankind the deadly defamations of the names of God and of his character that come to light as a result of the misunderstandings men have about the doctrine of vicarious atonement.

They do not understand what honest-to-goodness atonement really means. According to cosmic law, Jesus cannot atone for your sins. Only you can atone for your sins. And Jesus cannot make your decisions for you any more than anyone else can make your decisions for you. In the final analysis, each one has to make his own decisions.

God has set his laws in motion, and in so doing he has conveyed to all of us the ritual of free will. Through our use of the free will he bequeathed to us, we are able to receive the true salvation of Jesus Christ, which is the gift of the Christ consciousness. God planned this from the beginning. He foreknew that one day we would exercise our free will to return to him in the full glory of the ascension.

You see, even God does not ordain our comings and our goings. And it is not enough for God to merely will your destiny for you, for he has already willed the destiny of every human being. Only *we* can decide when we will have our victories—and when we will have our defeats, God forbid.

We will not win our salvation through our worship of Jesus or any other Master, but we will win it through the Master within, who is given to us directly from God. This Master is our own Holy Christ Self. Our Holy Christ Self descends from the Godhead, from the I AM Presence and the Causal Body with its concentric globes of fire that represent our "treasures in heaven, where neither moth nor rust doth corrupt and where thieves do not break through nor steal."[27]

At the time we were born, when the universal flame was lit in the chalice of our heart and it began to beat with the rhythm of the Holy Spirit, we were given individual life, consciousness and energy. Then the descending dove of the Holy Spirit came down upon the Holy Christ Self, individualized for each of us. It descended along the crystal cord until the threefold flame of life was anchored in the heart of the newborn babe.

This threefold flame, thank God, has been seen not only by clairvoyants but by people who have seen it with their naked eye. There have been cases where people have actually looked through an opening in the chest of a man during surgery and seen the threefold flame within the patient's heart.

I want you to understand that many of the great problems that we have in the human cauldron, seething with human emotions, stem from people's addictions to their own ideas. That's what makes conveying the eternal truths so difficult.

I would not be working as hard as I do merely for dollars. I am working as hard as I do for the saving of souls. I am not working for fame. Had I chosen fame and fortune, I would have gone into business or politics.

The point is, each one of us has free will. Any one of us could choose to be here or not to be here in the service of God. I am here because I want to be engaged in the work of the Good Shepherd. Our work enunciates the ancient alphabets of the Spirit that go back to the priesthood of Melchizedek. Of Christ it was said, "Thou art a priest forever after the order of Melchizedek."[28]

Those who are willing to give everything to the Godhead, to surrender completely to God, may be accepted into that order. I use the word *may* because it is not easy to qualify oneself for a level-one entrée into the priesthood of Melchizedek. Those who are members of that order are a type of Christ. And they bear the burden and the light of their Christhood.

And so, I have presented you with some thoughts on Christmas in July, a Christmas you must keep forever, a Christmas that will resurrect the light of the Christ Mass upon the planetary body.

One more thought comes to mind that shows how much God loves every one of us. Some of you are aware that El Morya was embodied as the Irish poet and lyricist Thomas Moore. He was quite popular in his day for his skill as a drawing-room singer. You may be interested in hearing, then, a little bit of the story of his writing of the song "Believe Me, If All Those Endearing Young Charms."

Thomas Moore and the beautiful daughter of an aristocrat fell in love, although they never married. Each held back from the relationship—Thomas because he was the son of an Irish grocer, the girl because an attack of smallpox had left one side of her face disfigured. The poor girl kept her disfigurement from Thomas. Although she still attended his singing performances, she would sit in the shadows and cover her face with her fan.

When Thomas discovered her secret, he composed a new song under divine inspiration. He performed it one night at a gathering attended by the prince regent. Contrary to the accepted ways of etiquette, he turned his back on royalty and faced the girl he loved to sing to her this tender song:

> Believe me, if all those endearing young charms,
>   Which I gaze on so fondly to-day,
> Were to change by to-morrow, and fleet in my arms,
>   Like fairy-gifts fading away,
> Thou wouldst still be adored, as this moment thou art,
>   Let thy loveliness fade as it will,
> And around the dear ruin each wish of my heart
>   Would entwine itself verdantly still.

It is not while beauty and youth are thine own,
    And thy cheeks unprofaned by a tear,
That the fervour and faith of a soul can be known,
    To which time will but make thee more dear;
No, the heart that has truly loved never forgets,
    But as truly loves on to the close,
As the sun-flower turns on her god, when he sets,
    The same look which she turn'd when he rose.

The pathos of the Master-to-be! Thank you.

ॐ

୫ "Within this earthen vessel are bowers
and groves, and within it is the Creator:

Within this vessel are the seven oceans
and the unnumbered stars.

The touchstone and the jewel-appraiser
are within;

And within this vessel the Eternal
soundeth, and the spring wells up.

Kabir says: 'Listen to me, my Friend!
My beloved Lord is within.'"

—KABĪR

The Chart of
Your Divine Self

You have a unique spiritual destiny. One of the keys to fulfilling that destiny is understanding your divine nature and your relationship to God.

To help you understand this relationship, the Ascended Masters have designed the Chart of Your Divine Self, which they also refer to as the Tree of Life. The Chart is a portrait of you and the God within you, a diagram of yourself—past, present and future.

THE I AM PRESENCE AND CAUSAL BODY

The Chart of Your Divine Self has three figures, corresponding to the Three Persons of the Trinity and the Divine Mother. The upper figure corresponds to the Father (who is one with the Mother) and represents your I AM Presence. The I AM Presence is the Presence of God individualized for each of us. It is your personalized I AM THAT I AM, the name of God revealed to Moses at Mount Sinai.

Your I AM Presence is surrounded by seven concentric spheres of rainbow light that make up your Causal Body. The spheres of your Causal Body are the storehouse of everything that is real and permanent about you. They contain the records of the virtuous acts you have performed to the glory of God and the blessing of man through your many incarnations on earth.

No two Causal Bodies are exactly alike because their shimmering spheres reflect the unique spiritual attainment of the soul. The particular attributes you have developed in your previous lives determine the gifts and talents you will be born with in your succeeding lives. These talents are sealed in your Causal Body and made available to you through your Higher Self.

THE HOLY CHRIST SELF

Your Higher Self, or Holy Christ Self, is depicted as the middle figure in the Chart of Your Divine Self. Your Holy Christ Self is your inner teacher, guardian and dearest friend. He is also the voice of conscience that speaks within your heart and soul. He divides the way between good and evil within you, teaching you right from wrong.

Shown just above the head of the Holy Christ Self is the dove of the Holy Spirit descending in the benediction of the Father-Mother God.

The shaft of white light descending from the I AM Presence through the Holy Christ Self to the lower figure in the Chart is the crystal cord. In Ecclesiastes, it is referred to as the silver cord (Eccles. 12:6). Through this "umbilical cord" flows a cascading stream of God's light, life and consciousness. This stream of life empowers you to think, feel, reason, experience life and grow spiritually.

YOUR DIVINE SPARK AND FOUR LOWER BODIES

The energy of your crystal cord nourishes and sustains the flame of God that is ensconced in the secret chamber of your heart. This flame is called the threefold flame or divine spark. It is literally a spark of sacred fire from God's own heart.

The threefold flame has three "plumes." These plumes embody the three primary attributes of God and correspond to the Trinity. The white-fire core from which the threefold flame springs represents the Mother.

As you visualize the threefold flame within you, see the blue plume on your left. It embodies God's power and corresponds to the Father. The yellow plume, in the center, embodies God's wisdom and corresponds to the Son. The pink plume, on your right, embodies God's love and corresponds to the Holy Spirit. By accessing the power, wisdom and love anchored in your threefold flame, you can fulfill your reason for being.

The lower figure in the Chart represents your soul. Your soul is sheathed in four different "bodies," called the four lower bodies: (1) the etheric body, (2) the mental body, (3) the desire body and (4) the physical body. These are the vehicles your soul uses in her journey on earth.

Your etheric body, also called the memory body, houses the blueprint of your identity. It also contains the memory of all that has ever transpired in your soul and all impulses you have ever sent out through your soul since you were created. Your mental body is the vessel of your cognitive faculties. When it is purified it can become the vessel of the Mind of God.

The desire body, also called the emotional body, houses your higher and lower desires and records your emotions.

Your physical body is the miracle of flesh and blood that enables your soul to progress in the material universe.

The lower figure in the chart corresponds to the Holy Spirit, for your soul and four lower bodies are intended to be the temple of the Holy Spirit. The lower figure is enveloped in the violet flame—the transmutative, spiritual fire of the Holy Spirit. You can invoke the violet flame daily to purify your four lower bodies and consume negative thoughts, negative feelings and negative karma.

Surrounding the violet flame is the tube of light, which descends from your I AM Presence in answer to your call. It is a cylinder of white light that sustains a forcefield of protection around you twenty-four hours a day as long as you maintain your harmony.

The Divine Mother focuses her energy within us through the sacred fire of God that rises as a fountain of light through our chakras. *Chakras* is a Sanskrit term for the spiritual centers in the etheric body. Each chakra regulates the flow of energy to a different part of the body. The seven major chakras are positioned along the spinal column from the base of the spine to the crown.

THE DESTINY OF THE SOUL

The soul is the living potential of God. The purpose of the soul's evolution on earth is to perfect herself under the tutelage of her Holy Christ Self and to return to God through union with her I AM Presence in the ritual of the ascension. The soul may go through numerous incarnations before she is perfected and is thereby worthy to reunite with God.

What happens to the soul between incarnations? When the soul concludes a lifetime on earth, the I AM Presence withdraws the crystal cord. The threefold flame returns to the heart of the Holy Christ Self, and the soul gravitates to the highest level of consciousness to which she has attained in all of her incarnations.

If the soul merits it, between embodiments she is schooled in the retreats, or spiritual homes, of the Ascended Masters in the heaven-world. There she studies with angels and masters of wisdom who have gained mastery in their fields of specialization.

The ascension is the culmination of lifetimes of the soul's service to life. In order for the soul to attain this ultimate union with God she must become one with her Holy Christ Self, she must balance (pay the debt for) at least 51 percent of her karma, and she must fulfill her mission on earth according to her divine plan. When your soul ascends back to God you will become an Ascended Master, free from the round of karma and rebirth, and you will receive the crown of everlasting life.

Notes

CHAPTER ONE *Christ in the Heart of Man*

Title page quotations:

Kigen Dōgen, Japanese Zen Buddhist master.

Jesus, early Christian saying, taken from G. R. S. Mead, *Fragments of a Faith Forgotten* (New Hyde Park, N.Y.: University Books, n.d.), p. 596.

1. John 10:16.
2. John 14:2, 3.
3. I John 4:8, 16.
4. Matt. 24:23; Mark 13:21; Luke 17:21, 23.
5. Matt. 7:12; Luke 6:31.
6. Paramahansa Yogananda, *Autobiography of a Yogi* (1946; reprint, Los Angeles: Self-Realization Fellowship, 1977), p. 349.
7. James 2:23.
8. Luke 23:39–43.
9. Job 1:21.
10. I Cor. 15:51, 52.

11. Matt. 24:29–31; Mark 13:24–27; Luke 21:25–28; I Thess. 4:16, 17; Rev. 1:7.

12. Matt. 25:32, 33.

13. Matt. 5:14.

14. John 12:32.

15. Heb. 12:29.

16. Dan. 3:10–29.

17. John 1:1–3, 10.

18. Col. 2:9.

19. Eccles. 1:2, 14.

20. John 3:19–21.

21. II Cor. 3:18.

22. Robert Browning, *Pippa Passes,* pt. 1.

23. Matt. 7:16, 20.

24. See the Bhagavad Gītā.

25. Matt. 6:22, 23.

CHAPTER TWO *How to Develop the Christ Consciousness*

Title page quotation:

Jalaluddin Rumi, Sufi poet and mystic, *Mathnawī* II, "Moses and the Shepherd."

1. Rom. 6:6; Eph. 4:22–24; Col. 3:9, 10.

2. I Cor. 8:8.

3. Gal. 3:1, 3.

4. Rom. 14:13.

5. Matt. 14:23; Mark 6:46; Luke 6:12; 9:28.

6. Exod. 33:20.

7. Matt. 6:6.

8. I Cor. 14:32.

9. Matt. 14:13.

10. Eph. 6:11–17.

11. John 15:18, 19; 17:14.

12. While Risë Stevens, mezzo-soprano, was singing Orpheo's aria of lamentation at the foot of the Acropolis, she "lost all touch with reality" and felt herself in ancient Greece, "mentally and physically" living a former life in which she had acted on that very stage. Later she wrote about the incident, saying she finished the aria as if she were in a trance and "fell prostrate on the body of Euridice." It took five minutes of thunderous applause to bring her back to the present. See Kyle Crichton, *Subway to the Met: Risë Stevens' Story* (Garden City, N.Y.: Doubleday & Company, 1959), pp. 237–38.

13. John 3:8.

14. Matt. 13:24–30.

15. Matt. 21:12, 13; Mark 11:15–17; Luke 19:45, 46; John 2:13–16.

16. John 2:17.

17. Isa. 8:19.

CHAPTER THREE *Eternal Christmas in July*

Title page quotations:

Paramahansa Yogananda, *Self-Realization Magazine* and *Metaphysical Meditations.*

Teresa of Avila, *The Interior Castle* 4.1.7.

1. John 3:16.

2. John 1:3.

3. Matt. 24:23; Mark 13:21; Luke 17:21, 23.

4. Matt. 25:40.

5. Acts 10:9–48; 11:1–18.

6. The *pranam* is a respectful form of greeting used throughout India in which one places the palms together in front of the chest and nods the head slightly.

7. The world headquarters of The Summit Lighthouse was located at La Tourelle in Colorado Springs, Colorado, from 1966 to 1976. The headquarters is now located at the Royal Teton Ranch in Montana.

8. Matt. 7:16, 20.

9. John 4:14; Rev. 21:6; 22:1, 17.

10. I Cor. 13:11.

11. Matt. 10:7–19.

12. I John 4:16, 12.

13. In Babylonian mythology, Tiamat is the female principle of chaos. She takes the form of a dragon.

14. John 15:12, 13.

15. Fred Eppsteiner, ed., *The Path of Compassion: Writings on Socially Engaged Buddhism,* 2d ed. (Berkeley, Calif.: Parallax Press and Buddhist Peace Fellowship, 1988), p. 19.

16. Juan Mascaró, trans., *The Dhammapada: The Path of Perfection* (London: Penguin Books, 1973), p. 35.

17. Noel Langley, *Edgar Cayce on Reincarnation* (New York: Warner Books, 1967), pp. 184, 186, 197–98.

18. II Kings 2:9–15.

19. John 3:30; Luke 3:16.

20. Luke 1:39–44, 35.

21. Matt. 17:9–13.

22. Matt. 14:1–11; Mark 6:14–28.

23. Matt. 11:11.

24. Matt. 3:3; Mark 1:2, 3; Luke 3:3, 4; Isa. 40:3.

25. Mal. 4:5, 6.

26. Heb. 13:8.

27. Matt. 6:20.

28. Heb. 5:5–10; 6:20; 7.

Quotation, p. 91:

　　Kabīr, Indian mystical poet, *Songs of Kabīr* , song 1.101, trans. Rabindranath Tagore (1977; reprint, York Beach, Maine: Samuel Weiser, 1991), p. 52.

Glossary

Akashic records. The impressions of all that has ever transpired in the physical universe, recorded in an etheric substance and dimension known as akasha. These records can be read by those with developed soul faculties.

Ascended Masters. Enlightened spiritual beings who once lived on earth, fulfilled their reason for being and have ascended, or reunited with God. The Ascended Masters are the true teachers of mankind. They direct the spiritual evolution of all devotees of God and guide them back to their Source.

Ascension. A spiritual acceleration of consciousness that takes place at the natural conclusion of one's final lifetime on earth whereby the soul reunites with God and is free from the round of karma and rebirth. *See also* pp. 96, 97.

Astral plane. The lowest vibrating frequency of time and space; the repository of mankind's thoughts and feelings, conscious and unconscious.

Avatar. From Sanskrit *avatara,* literally "descent." A Hindu term for an incarnation of God on earth.

Body elemental. A being of nature who serves the soul as an unseen but constant companion and physician through all the soul's incarnations.

Carnal mind. The human ego, human intellect and human will; the animal nature of man.

Causal Body. Interpenetrating spheres of light surrounding each one's I AM Presence at spiritual levels. The spheres of the Causal Body contain the records of the virtuous acts we have performed to the glory of God and the blessing of man through our many incarnations on earth. *See also* pp. 92–94.

Chart of Your Divine Self. *See* pp. 92–97.

Christ Self. *See* Holy Christ Self.

Crystal cord. The stream of God's light, life and consciousness that nourishes and sustains the soul and her four lower bodies. Also called the silver cord. *See also* pp. 94–95, 97.

Decree. A dynamic form of spoken prayer used by students of the Ascended Masters to direct God's light into individual and world conditions.

Desire body. *See* Four lower bodies.

Dictation. The messages of the Ascended Masters, archangels and other advanced spiritual beings delivered through the agency of the Holy Spirit by a Messenger of the Great White Brotherhood.

Divine spark. *See* Threefold flame.

El Morya. The Ascended Master who is the teacher and sponsor of the Messengers Mark L. Prophet and Elizabeth Clare Prophet and the founder of The Summit Lighthouse.

Etheric body. *See* Four lower bodies.

Four lower bodies. The four sheaths surrounding the soul; the vehicles the soul uses in her journey on earth: the etheric, or memory, body; the mental body; the desire, or emotional, body; the physical body.

The etheric body houses the blueprint of the soul's identity and contains the memory of all that has ever transpired in the soul and all impulses she has ever sent out. The mental body is the vessel of the cognitive faculties; when purified, it can become the vessel of the Mind of God. The desire body houses the higher and lower desires and records the emotions. The physical body is the miracle of flesh and blood that enables the soul to progress in the material universe.

God Presence. *See* I AM Presence.

Great White Brotherhood. A spiritual fraternity of Ascended Masters, archangels and other advanced spiritual beings. The term "white" refers not to race but to the aura of white light that surrounds these immortals. The Great White Brotherhood works with earnest seekers of every race, religion and walk of life to assist humanity. The Brotherhood also includes certain unascended disciples of the Ascended Masters.

Holy Christ Self. The Higher Self; our inner teacher, guardian, friend and advocate before God; the Universal Christ individualized for each of us. *See also* pp. 94, 96, 97.

I AM Presence. The Presence of God, the I AM THAT I AM, individualized for each of us. *See also* pp. 93, 96–97.

Karma. Sanskrit, meaning act, action, work or deed. The consequences of one's thoughts, words and deeds of this life and previous lives; the law of cause and effect, which decrees that whatever we do comes full circle to our doorstep for resolution. The law of karma necessitates the soul's reincarnation so that she can pay the debt for, or "balance," her misuses of God's light, energy and consciousness.

Light. The universal radiance and energy of God.

Memory body. *See* Four lower bodies.

Messenger. One trained by an Ascended Master to receive and deliver the teachings, messages and prophecies of the Great White Brotherhood for a people and an age.

Physical body. *See* Four lower bodies.

Retreat. The spiritual home of an Ascended Master or heavenly being. Retreats are located chiefly in the heaven-world.

Saint Germain. The Ascended Master who is Hierarch of the Aquarian Age and sponsor of the United States of America.

Serapis Bey. The Ascended Master who prepares and trains candidates for the ascension. Serapis Bey is the hierarch of the Ascension Temple, a retreat located in the heaven-world at Luxor, Egypt.

The Summit Lighthouse. An outer organization of the Great White Brotherhood. Mark L. Prophet founded The Summit Lighthouse in 1958 under the direction of the Ascended Master El Morya to publish the teachings of the Ascended Masters.

Threefold flame. The divine spark, the flame of God ensconced within the secret chamber of the heart; the soul's point of contact with her Supreme Source. *See also* pp. 95, 97.

Mark L. Prophet and Elizabeth Clare Prophet are pioneers in modern spirituality. In 1958, Mark founded The Summit Lighthouse to publish the teachings of the Ascended Masters, the saints and sages of East and West who have attained union with God. Among the Prophets' published works are such classics as *The Lost Years of Jesus, The Lost Teachings of Jesus, The Human Aura* and *Saint Germain On Alchemy*. The Prophets have also lectured widely throughout the United States and internationally.

In 1970, the Prophets founded Montessori International, a school based on the principles of the acclaimed educator Dr. Maria Montessori, to give children a learning environment in which they could best realize their inner potential. In 1971, they founded Summit University for those who wanted to gain a deeper understanding of the teachings of the Ascended Masters and study a mystical approach to the world's religions.

Mark passed on in 1973 and Elizabeth carries on their work. She lives in Montana at the Royal Teton Ranch, home of a spiritual community where she conducts conferences and workshops. The Summit Lighthouse has 220 study centers around the world.

Elizabeth Clare Prophet's lectures and workshops on angels, the aura, soul mates, prophecy, spiritual psychology, reincarnation, the mystical paths of the world's religions and other topics are broadcast on more than 200 cable TV stations throughout the United States. She has been featured on NBC's "Ancient Prophecies" and she has talked about her work on "Donahue," "Larry King Live!" "Nightline," "Sonya Live" and "CNN & Company."

Other titles from
SUMMIT UNIVERSITY PRESS

The Lost Years of Jesus

The Lost Teachings of Jesus
BOOK 1 *Missing Texts • Karma and Reincarnation*
BOOK 2 *Mysteries of the Higher Self*
BOOK 3 *Keys to Self-Transcendence*
BOOK 4 *Finding the God Within*

The Human Aura

Saint Germain On Alchemy

Forbidden Mysteries of Enoch

Dossier on the Ascension

The Science of the Spoken Word

Prayer and Meditation

Summit University Press titles are available directly
from the publisher or from fine bookstores everywhere,
including Barnes and Noble, B. Dalton Bookseller,
Borders and Waldenbooks.

For a free catalog of books and tapes by Mark L.
Prophet and Elizabeth Clare Prophet or for information
about conferences, workshops, Summit Lighthouse study
centers or cable TV programs in your area, contact
The Summit Lighthouse, Dept. 457, Box 5000,
Corwin Springs, Montana 59030-5000 U.S.A. Telephone
1-800-245-5445 (outside the U.S.A., 406-848-9891).
Fax 1-800-221-8307 (outside the U.S.A., 406-848-9866).
Or visit our Web site at http://www.tsl.org